BEDSIT LAND

Manchester University Press

BEDSIT LAND

The strange worlds
of Soft Cell

PATRICK CLARKE

Manchester University Press

The right of Patrick Clarke to be identified as the author of this work has been asserted in accordance with the Copyright, Designs and Patents Act 1988.

Published by Manchester University Press
Oxford Road, Manchester, M13 9PL

www.manchesteruniversitypress.co.uk

British Library Cataloguing-in-Publication Data
A catalogue record for this book is available from the British Library

ISBN 978 1 5261 7356 0 paperback

First published 2024

The publisher has no responsibility for the persistence or accuracy of URLs for any external or third-party internet websites referred to in this book, and does not guarantee that any content on such websites is, or will remain, accurate or appropriate.

Typeset
by Cheshire Typesetting Ltd, Cuddington, Cheshire

CONTENTS

Preface   *page* vi

Introduction   1

1 Lubbock's Day   5

2 The Yorkshire Vortex   22

3 Memorabilia   55

4 Art terrorism   74

5 Da dun dun   86

6 *Top of the Pops*   105

7 I shook them up and I gave them hell   121

8 Soho   153

9 We could go out to dinner but we're always on
  drugs   186

Epilogue   220

Acknowledgements   223

Notes   226

Index   241

PREFACE

CONTENTS

When I was born, in 1994, Soft Cell had been defunct for over a decade. They came into my life, as I assume they did for most people my age and younger, via 'Tainted Love', perhaps heard on some oldies compilation or another, or on the playlist at a retro night in a student indie bar.

It was not until I was assigned to write an article as part of my job at *The Quietus*, an interview with the band and their collaborators to mark the fortieth anniversary of debut album *Non-Stop Erotic Cabaret* in 2021, that I came to realise quite how extraordinary they really were. At that point I was the only staff writer at a severely under-resourced DIY publication, so my work often required me to delve deep into the world of a band I might not otherwise be acquainted with, getting as clear a picture as I could as quickly as possible, writing it up to a strict deadline and then moving on. Soft Cell were supposed to be one such band, yet the further I got from that piece, the more often I found myself drawn back to them. When tasked with looking beyond the pop veneer of 'Tainted Love', I had found a seemingly endless well of material in which Soft Cell were blending the sordid and the euphoric, cultures high and low with no concern for arbitrary distinctions between the two, a wicked sense of humour and a raw, fraying soul. It nestled deep within my psyche.

This book began life as an extension of that *Quietus* article, drawing on new interviews with the band, their collaborators, their friends and occasionally their foes, as well as archival accounts. As it evolved, however, what also emerged was a desire to dig deeper and deeper into those wider worlds through which they travelled: the faded camp glamour of the seaside where both Marc Almond and Dave Ball were born, the radical transgression of the art school at which they met, the glitz and grimness of British showbiz, the explosive release of Northern Soul, the unhinged hedonism of early 1980s pre-AIDS New York, the early days of truly DIY labels, the magnetic sleaze of Soho and the extraordinary collective of experimental musicians that descended around the offices of their manager Stevo's chaotic label Some Bizzare. As a result, I have spoken to experts too, historians of particular places and times, and biographers of the singular figures which ruled them, as well as people who, though they might never have intersected with Marc Almond or Dave Ball, also experienced these worlds first hand.

I am aware of course that *Bedsit Land* is a book written from a distance, by a writer who was not only not around at the time of Soft Cell's first phase but not in existence. I have tried to use that to my advantage, however, and to approach these worlds with the same open-mindedness and exploratory instincts that Almond and Ball employed to such effect – to approach them with virgin eyes and ears, without preconception. In the interest of conciseness, I have chosen to close the narrative with the end of Soft Cell's first 'era', their 1984 hiatus, rather than exploring their later reformation in 2000 and their ongoing work since 2018. Given the band has never really 'split', beginnings and endings are essentially arbitrary. Nevertheless, the line had to be drawn somewhere.

As with any subject forty years in the past, recollections from those interviewed often vary and fine details become hazy, while some direct accounts that would doubtless have been valuable to me were, for one reason or another, unavailable. Some of the figures who helped shaped Soft Cell's worlds are no longer with us, such as the pioneering New York DJ Anita Sarko, their fellow student Frank Tovey of the equally groundbreaking Fad Gadget, as well as great swathes of the queer community who were taken by the AIDS epidemic. Some, like Cindy Ecstasy or Soft Cell's early third member Steven Griffith, have simply disappeared off the map completely. Nevertheless, I hope that the picture I present through this book is one of considerable depth, drawing as it does from over sixty separate interviews conducted since 2021 and extensive archive material.

Though I have done my utmost to simultaneously tell a clear and concise narrative of the band themselves that I can use as my guide through these strange worlds, I do not view this project as a straightforward biography. Instead, the aim is to broaden the scope, to present Soft Cell not just as the one-hit pop stars they are so often maligned as, but as a band who contain multitudes.

INTRODUCTION

In Florida, a small plane is grounded because of the weight of the rare soul records that a precocious teenage boy is insisting he take with him on a flight to the Caribbean. In London, a boa constrictor escapes from its cage and slithers out into the rainy night, past the strip clubs and clip joints of Soho and down into the sewers, never to be seen again. Not far away, in student digs, a trainee double bassist awakes screaming, convinced that he is hearing the voice of God. In Blackpool, a drunk stumbling from a casino in the early morning questions reality as a herd of elephants stomp their way down the Pleasure Beach in the frigid morning air. Two student performance artists in Leeds are hauled into court, having attempted to execute budgies and mice to the tune of 'Camptown Races', stopped only by a riot among horrified onlookers. Celebrants at a Fourth of July rooftop party in New York barbecue hot dogs, finish their meals, then head downstairs into a dingy basement for a mass orgy around a bathtub that has been transported symbolically for the occasion from America's opposite coast. A music fan in an Alicante bullfighting ring decants mescaline into their wine, shortly before all hell breaks loose.

These are snapshots of just a few of the strange worlds through which Marc Almond and Dave Ball passed in Soft Cell's brief first phase of existence. A band who were attracted to weirdness, and to whom weirdness was attracted, they were surrounded both by design and by chance by cultural curiosities and extremities of all types. Though not even four years elapsed between the duo's first self-released EP and their glorious implosion in 1984, the music they recorded in that time period is breathtaking in its scope. It is the product of transgressive student performance art, the giddy euphoria of disco, underground Soho sleaze, diversions in Spanish flamenco and French chanson, raunchy end-of-the-pier music hall, no wave's sonic extremity, the melodrama of Northern Soul, the flamboyance of Weimar expressionism, the futuristic visions of Krautrock. And yet it is entirely their own, built from the strange new elements that are created when one of those influences reacts against another.

This is not, however, the way Soft Cell are often perceived – at least not by anyone other than the devoted. To most, they are familiar due to their debut album and a brief string of pop hits in 1981, mainly the gargantuan 'Tainted Love', a song so monstrously successful that it overshadows them to this day. 'Tainted Love' is a work of pop genius, a meeting of Krautrock and Northern Soul so addictive that it would ultimately be ruinous, yet pop is just one of Soft Cell's many faces. Comparing them to the other British groups who crashed ashore on the first wave of synth pop – Orchestral Manoeuvres in the Dark, Human

League, Depeche Mode – what sticks out the most is really their lack of polish and their frayed edges, their embrace of wonkiness and wit, sleaze and spikiness at the expense of slickness.

Had 'Tainted Love' never been released, Soft Cell might have been canonised – along the same lines as their American idols Suicide, their Leeds Polytechnic classmate Fad Gadget or their Sheffield forebears Cabaret Voltaire – as trailblazing cult heroes. Their status as Britain's first synth duo would have provided the blueprint that the likes of Pet Shop Boys and Eurythmics could then deploy to pop stardom of their own, but Soft Cell should have been too wonky and uncommercial to reach such levels themselves. They might well have been more comfortable, freer to embrace all those left-field influences without the interference of a record label so keen to milk them for hits. They might not have buckled under the pressure and burnt themselves out within just a few years. Yet because of the surprise success of 'Tainted Love', Soft Cell were essentially denied the narrative that would have properly befitted them, like a planet knocked into an elliptical orbit by an interstellar collision.

Fame, of course, still had plenty of benefits, such as the way it coloured their trip to New York in 1981. At that time the city was at the crest of a wave, emerging from the economic turmoil and plummeting living standards of the 1970s, but not yet subject to the skyrocketing of rents that would follow later in the decade. Nor had the AIDS epidemic – which hit New York particularly badly – reached anything like its full destructive force. Culture was still booming on every front in a seemingly endless array of clubs of all sizes and, as the forerunners of the so-called 'Second British Invasion' of UK pop stars, Soft Cell were on every guestlist. Their hoovering up of culture was thrust into overdrive as they dived headfirst through all those open doors. What they found inside, whether a bacchanalian underground sex club or a bombastic mega-disco, was not just to add to their already expansive array of influences but to charge their music with a cascading energy that would maintain them through three studio albums, a remix LP and a VHS so controversial that they were raided by the vice squad.

Their career was to be shaped by those two forces – the primal pull of artistic expression constantly being buffeted and occasionally blown off course by the turbulence of fame. In response, the pull towards their art grew stronger in an effort to break free, causing their work to evolve in triple time. In just a few years they arrived at the dark crescendo of *This Last Night ... in Sodom*, their final, sprawling masterpiece.

It is worth remembering, of course, that there were two human beings at the eye of this storm. For Marc Almond and Dave Ball, who had initially formed Soft Cell simply as a way to soundtrack the former's student art pieces, the dramatic peaks and troughs that make Soft Cell so intriguing also came with mental anguish and increasingly prolific substance abuse that would contribute just as much to their early demise as the identity crisis that many performance artists experience when they hit the big time. And yet, this is the story we are presented with – of a band who never stopped morphing and mutating, despite the pressures on them to do the opposite, and who responded to stardom by subverting it at every turn, ploughing on relentlessly in their journey through the world's dark underbellies, no matter the cost.

Chapter 1
LUBBOCK'S DAY

For an upper-class Victorian lady, a pair of gloves was the embodiment of sophistication, a symbol that she did not have to sully her hands with manual labour. If she were respectable, she would never leave the house without them, and when in company would remove them only when dining.[1]

When that upper-class Victorian lady arrived at the seaside, it is said she would purposefully leave her gloves behind her on the train.

Dr Kathryn Ferry, historian of the seaside: The seaside has always had a certain air about it, a sense that you can get away with things on the fringes of the country, in that liminal space between the land and the sea. The normal rules don't apply.[2]

Perhaps it was only from the English coast that a band like Soft Cell could emerge. Dave Ball, from Blackpool, and Marc Almond, from Southport, were at their best when they wrote the soundtrack to the fringes. This is usually linked with the surreal bacchanalia of the club scene that they threw themselves into during their rise to fame in the 1980s – the non-stop erotic cabaret for which their debut album was to be named – but really fringe culture had been around them from the start.

Marc Almond, Soft Cell: I think a listener to Soft Cell can get a sense we were both from Lancashire seaside towns. There is an element of seaside postcard trash in our music, terrible variety entertainers and cabaret duos playing in seaside bars singing club songs to a Bontempi organ and a singer out of tune giving it too much in a bad outfit and makeup. A sinister scary camp.[3]

Consider a character like the protagonist of 'Bedsitter', skint, alone and unsatisfied, the banal grind of the everyday juxtaposed with the thrilling, financially ruinous parallel world of the night. The bedsitter's release might be found in 'clubland', not the seaside, but he could just as easily be imagined as a worker pining for the days he could let loose on the Pleasure Beach. Clubland and the seaside are merely different regions of the same alternative dimension.

Dave Ball, Soft Cell: 'Bedsitter' wasn't really written about Blackpool or Southport, but it could have been.[4]

The seaside is not the same thing as the coast because it is a concept of human creation. In 1626 a mineral spring was discovered in Scarborough, and the first resort was built around it.[5] By the eighteenth century, rich Georgians would be sent to such places by their doctors for the supposed benefits of a freezing cold, early morning ocean swim. Entrepreneurs began setting up shop in what were then small fishing communities to start catering for these rich visitors and so the focus shifted from health to leisure. As the Industrial Revolution brought both steam-powered trains and an explosion of industry, so too did it bring hordes of holidaymakers from factories, farms and mills. 'Wakes Weeks', where industry would temporarily shut down to allow workers to take a break, would be staggered among different industrial towns.[6] All of Halifax would descend on the beaches one weekend, all of Bolton the next.

In 1871 the Bank Holidays Act first designated Easter Monday, Whit Monday, the first Monday in August and Boxing Day as days off. So popular was Sir John Lubbock, the politician who spearheaded the act, that there was a campaign to name the August holiday 'Lubbock's Day'.

News of the World, 1871: Blessings on the head of Sir John Lubbock, who invented a decent excuse for holidays to Englishmen […] we certainly did wish that some great inventive genius could discover a reason why the people should not work all the year round.[7]

The seaside had also been an otherworldly place before that. Sixty years earlier the Prince Regent and later King George IV transformed his seaside villa in Brighton into the decadent faux-oriental dream palace that still stands today, and filled it with art and extravagant parties.[8] Now that spirit had spilled over into the masses. On heaving beaches there was a giddy maximalism, hardworking people reinventing themselves as creatures of leisure, free to create entire new personas, if only for a long weekend.

7

The throngs of entertainers that followed were all too happy to play on that theme. Popular comedy sketches would concern a stuffy or downtrodden character adopting a new and flamboyant persona, only to receive their come-uppance when they ran into someone from back home on the promenade. Humorous postcards would depict young couples exasperated when they ran into the prying relatives they had come to the seaside to avoid.

Dr Kathryn Ferry: On holiday you've got a different backdrop. You've left your head behind, and you can be a different person. The seaside has always had that element to it. I guess that's why in films and stories, when people elope, they go off to some dodgy hotel in Brighton and sign in as Mr and Mrs Smith.

By the late 1950s, when Marc Almond and Dave Ball were born, the seaside was booming again. With two world wars still fresh in the memory, a nostalgia for the time before them was emerging in response. Victorian-style music hall and variety shows were still huge, and audiences were large enough to draw the biggest names in the country. Through the subsequent two decades, however, those rich enough started to holiday abroad and the clientele began to grow less affluent. Poorer audiences meant less renowned entertainers and less investment. By the time Almond and Ball were in their early teens, the glamour had begun to fade, and the energy had begun to get stranger.

Lubbock's Day

Dr Kathryn Ferry: There was still this desire among people going to the seaside for their holidays to have that razzmatazz, that bit of old-fashioned drama, the variety shows, the dancers, the comedies.

Almond and Ball were natives, not visitors, to the seaside. As a result, they were intertwined with their towns' respective spirits, able to observe the holidaymakers as they came and went. For Ball, growing up in Blackpool, even afternoon youth discos were accompanied by scantily clad go-go dancers. As a child he made pocket money from 'bagging' – waiting at the coach stop with a cart to carry arriving tourists' luggage to their guest house in exchange for a tip. Later he sold lottery tickets from a kiosk on the promenade and ice cream on the pier. His musical debut was as a DJ, purchasing a strobe light and hand-crafting a valve amplifier after school for six months, before taking his 'Smile Disco Show' across town.

Dave Ball: We'd do school discos and then also play my dad's masonic dances. We'd play pop, but then we'd also have to play all these waltzes and quicksteps. It was very strange. It was a very homemade effort, really. My dad worked [in telecommunications] for the GPO [General Post Office] so he was in the world of electronics. He used to build fruit machines for a friend of his who had an arcade on the Golden Mile, so in our garage there were loads of machines in different states of repair, all kinds of components which I would borrow. My dad had showed me a lot about how to build amplifiers and how to solder things. I was always very interested in electronics and how electricity works. He was always very insistent. When I wanted an electric guitar, he said, 'If you're going to play around with electricity, you need to know how it works.'

My dad had very little interest in music apart from when he'd play his Glenn Miller records at Christmas, but the electronic influence still really came from him. I was always interested in how things worked electronically, and then when synthesisers came into my life I never looked back.[9]

Almond suffered from bronchitis and asthma as a child, and his grandfather would take him on long walks along Southport beach in the hope that the salty air would provide respite – as if he were a miniature Georgian aristocrat. He spent later parts of his childhood in Leeds and Harrogate, but would always return to the coast for the duration of every summer. Around his fifteenth birthday, when his mother divorced his alcoholic and abusive father, they moved back for good, enrolling at a local grammar school, where he met Huw Feather. A year later the two would strike up a friendship at Southport Art College, which they both attended after leaving school; that friendship would go on to be one of the most significant of their lives. As Almond went on to stardom with Soft Cell, it was Feather who was initially the band's set designer and then their de facto creative director, helping to craft the visual identity that would intensify and solidify their impact.

Huw Feather: From day one, pop was my plug and connection to the world. I used to sing the charts to myself in bed to get myself to sleep, tapping out the rhythms. When I wasn't listening to records, I was also learning to be a magician, and I was an avid puppeteer and toy theatre enthusiast. My father had opened Southport's first legal casino in 1961 when the Gaming Act got repealed so he was very much interested in my card magic and sleight of hand. He'd take me to the Blackpool Convention for Magicians, which back then was like my Comic Con. I was nuts about fashion, too. I had a crazy great aunt in London who was a *bon vivant* and had been a model in the 1940s and 1950s. She used to throw open the doors of her wardrobe and instruct me on which designer was Chanel and which was Dior. She also took me to museums and encouraged me to look at various artists. I knew what I wanted to be and to do from the age of twelve, which was to be a theatre designer. My father dropped dead when I was fifteen. He had been against me being in the theatre, he wanted me to have a pension and look after my mum. But when he died my mum said, 'It's totally up to you.'

Marc arrived at grammar school when we were fourteen or fifteen, and then we both ended up at the art college. My friend Andy Dalglish was at the technical college next door, and the three of us were all in a theatre group together where I was doing the set design. I think I can see [the later Soft Cell visual style] in its nascent form in what we were doing there. Neon signs, advertising, musicals, dream sequences and drug trips.[10]

Almond worked on hook-a-duck, then bingo, at the Southport fairground, falling in love with its gaudy décor and colourful characters. When trying to pay back some money he had misappropriated from the theatre troupe for whom he had served as treasurer, he took a job at Southport Theatre where he operated the spotlight (Feather also found work there as a stagehand). His first job was a pantomime.

Marc Almond: The Southport Theatre was a strange carnival world where every day was some sexual assault by some low-on-the-bill pantomime variety act or seaside theatre empresario.[11]

Privy to the debauched afterparties that came along with the local theatre scene, Feather and Almond also began to explore Southport's queer side – albeit from a distance. There were the sand dunes on the outskirts of town, for instance, a popular spot for gay hook-ups that the teenagers dubbed 'fairyland'.

Huw Feather: The dunes are a huge part of Southport; people from the town are called Sandgrounders. They're the only undulation in our landscape; we're flat as a pancake otherwise. To actually get there you've got to go three train stops from Southport Central, so you're in no man's land, which is where all the 'bad behaviour' happened. We all grew up hearing, 'Keep away from the dunes, there's stuff going on there we don't want you to know about,' which, we found out later, is gay people cruising for trade.

I've always been bisexual, but in those days I didn't express it as that. I was 'straight', I had a girlfriend, blah blah blah, but Marc and I used to camp around with a hairdresser called Phillip who was quite clearly very gay. We'd call by after school, or meet him for a coffee, and just sit around, giggling and being outrageous. Nothing more, nothing less.

Ball, meanwhile, grew up both literally and figuratively in the shadow of Blackpool Tower. It was the tallest structure in the British Empire when it opened in 1894, five years after the Eiffel Tower, which it aped, and an imperious embodiment of all that era's swagger – a declaration that a northern English holiday town had the glamour and prestige to rival the belle époque.[12] By Ball's time, however, its main draw was the circus housed in the entertainment block down below.

Dave Ball: Norman Barrett was the famous ringmaster. It was when they still allowed them to have lions and tigers.[13]

Norman Barrett, Tower Circus ringmaster: I'm not knocking them, but a lot of ringmasters are just announcers, whereas I was an on-show director. Being a ringmaster isn't a job, it's a lifestyle. I was coming back into Blackpool one night at about three o'clock in the morning, and I had in the back of my Land Rover twelve budgerigars, four ballet-dancing pigeons, a boxer, a Yorkshire terrier and a clairvoyant hen. A policeman stopped me and said, 'What have you got in the back of the car?' I said, 'Twelve budgerigars, four ballet-dancing pigeons, a boxer, a Yorkshire terrier and a clairvoyant hen!'

We used to take the elephants to the sea in the morning, and thousands would come to see them exercising on the beach. Their trainer, Bobby Robertson, used to take the elephants up to the North Pier, leave them in a line, then run down to the Central Pier and shout to the elephants, 'Come down!' Then they would charge after him down the beach.[14]

Dave Ball: One Saturday morning when I was on the Golden Mile, selling lottery tickets from a little hut just opposite the Tower Circus, this dishevelled guy walked up to buy a ticket. He said he'd been in the casino all night. He was obviously still a bit pissed, and he said he was taking a stroll along the beach when he saw a herd of elephants coming towards him. I think he thought he was getting a bad bout of the DTs.[15]

Jackie Ratcliffe, ballet dancer and theatre performer: In 1975 I secured my first professional job, told fibs about my age, and then ran away from school. I joined a French roller-skating act and we performed the waterfall finale in the Tower Circus. The clowns would entertain the crowd while ring boys would roll up the matting. Once it was cleared, a circular section of the floor would rise up quite high. The ring would then start to fill with water and small fountains would start. The finale was two of us spinning by our necks as the fountains went up to full speed and height like a huge water-fall. To be honest, I can't remember how we'd get off stage at the end.[16]

Norman Barrett: The Tower Circus is the most beauti-ful circus building in the world, and when I worked there everything was the highest standard. We had trapeze artists, great jugglers, acrobats, always had the best going around. Charlie Cairoli was the big name, though. When he was there the place used to erupt. You wouldn't say you were going to the Tower Circus, you'd say, 'We're going to go and see Charlie tomorrow.'

Almond was heavily influenced by clowns of a more histori-cal kind, who he viewed as performance artists. This intensi-fied after he grew friendly with the troupe Clown Cavalcade after seeing a production of *Harlequinade* at the Southport Art Centre – a chaotic British slapstick adaptation of the

Italian *commedia dell'arte*, and the root of the modern pantomime. He and Feather performed a clown show of their own, too, touring the free festivals of the area.

Huw Feather: Marc was the white-faced clown, the character of Pierrot with a face painted in that mime artist kind of way, and I was Auguste, what we think of as a clown today with big makeup, red cheeks and an outlined lip, the bumbling buffoon.

Marc Almond: For me, the theatrical clowns, as opposed to circus clowns, were always preferable. I loved the white-faced, beautiful Harlequins, the Augustes with their spangly outfits that never seemed to be comical at all. I wished I could hide behind a face of white pan-stick makeup and wear glittering outfits. Years later, I became one such clown, as I stood on stage or in a television show in the spotlight, my clothes sparkling and my makeup just a little too pale – a ghost of all those past yearnings, fearful of revealing who I really was.[17]

It is no surprise that Soft Cell's earliest performances, after Almond and Ball met as art students at Leeds Polytechnic, were nothing if not a little clownish. They were essentially performance art shows consisting of tape loops, feedback and sound effects from Ball, and absurdity from Almond. For one piece called *Deterioration*, Almond donned a white wedding dress with fake blood pouring out of his mouth. He smashed glass photo frames to the floor, swallowed a bottle of pills and writhed around as Ball's sounds, sampled from a car crash, eventually morphed into Barbara Streisand's 'Memory'.

Tom Hardwick-Allen, clown and avant-garde musician: Experimental music and clowning ultimately seek radical presence, which often involves vulnerability. Doing things correctly can get in the way of this, as you fall back on what things should be, rather than what they could be. Experimental music often relies on intense listening, especially in free improv. Likewise, the clown feeds directly off its environment, and often an audience. Yet both experimental music and clowning often have a kind of disregard for the audience. It doesn't matter that a larger audience will likely not appreciate this or that piece of experimental music, the dialogue is with sound, not so much with the crowd. Meanwhile the clown is seen as an idiot, lesser than the real people watching, but it may well be the opposite way round – especially from the clown's perspective.

The experimental musician seeks particular material alignments that might offer a glimpse of transcendence. Both share a sideways logic that's more metonymic than it is intellectual. There's a sense of seeing things for what they really are, pushing things to extreme or ridiculous places to reveal pretences that we live by.[18]

Huw Feather: I can absolutely see a link between the *commedia dell'arte* and rock and roll. If you think about it, it's about telling a story or narrative on stage, using four set characters: Pierrot is the innocent who gets taken advantage of; Harlequin is sprightly, devilish and clever; Auguste is kind of an idiot; and then there's Columbine, who Harlequin, Auguste and Pierrot all fall for. I'm sure you could use those to view the different characters associated with frontmen, backing singers, bass, lead guitar or rhythm guitar.

Soft Cell were drawing on more straightforward influences too. At a gig at the Floral Hall in Southport, Almond was mesmerised by T. Rex frontman Marc Bolan, and would henceforth use his middle name Mark with an altered spelling, rather than his real forename, Peter, in tribute. Both he and Ball were spellbound when David Bowie (a literal clown turned pop star) performed 'Starman' on *Top of the Pops* in 1972 – Almond so much so that it would provide the direct model for his own performance of 'Tainted Love' on the show nine years later.

Dave Ball: Marc always said he wanted to have the same impact that David Bowie had had on him when he saw him do 'Starman'. Everyone of a certain age remembers seeing that and thinking, 'Wow, who's he?' With his blue acoustic guitar and red hair and no eyebrows, he looked like an alien. Then everyone at school the next day was saying, 'Who was that bloke? That David Bowie bloke?' Then by the next week they've all got David Bowie haircuts. He made it OK for boys to dye their hair and wear makeup, and I think Marc was in a way a continuation of that tradition.[19]

In general, though, popular rock bands were hard to come by in Blackpool – it was hard for 'proper' musicians to get a foothold in the seaside otherworld's strange, flipped hierarchy, where a budgie trainer might sell more tickets than T. Rex.

Dave Ball: Bands didn't play much in Blackpool often but the first I saw was Status Quo. That was when I first thought 'I want to be in a band, I want to do what they're doing.' Ten years later I was actually on the same stage. That was quite an amazing achievement for me, actually.[20]

He had better luck with Northern Soul. Every Friday and Saturday night at the Highland Room he would watch DJs Colin Curtis and Ian Levine, whose collection of thirty thousand vinyl records set them apart as rivals to the Wigan Casino.

Dave Ball: I'd been to junior discos at the Highland Room when I was a kid, but I wasn't allowed to go at that point because I was only about eleven. A few years later I started to sneak in. I just thought the whole thing was great. I liked the clothes, the baseball shirts and baggy trousers and flat shoes. It was really energetic. I'd always liked Motown and this was an extension of that, all these funny little record labels trying to emulate that success.[21]

This music spilled over to the tourist areas too, blasting out from the bass-heavy sound systems on the Pleasure Beach where he worked his succession of teenage jobs. One day, Ball and his colleagues at a beachside ice cream stall were waiting for the tide to go out so that they could set up shop, when he would have a different kind of musical experience. Usually, they would fill the time preparing cartons of orange juice using an ancient machine that burnt their hands, but this time there were no chores left.

Dave Ball: It was raining, and it was high tide, so there was no point going down to the beach. We were just stuck in the staff room at this factory, down one of the back alleys. One of the guys had an old-fashioned mono cassette player, and this cassette with a motorway sign on the cover. It was Kraftwerk's *Autobahn* and I was completely fascinated by it. For me, I thought if I was going to do music, there would be the Northern Soul influence and the Kraftwerk influence. I think there's a pretty obvious link to a certain single that we did later.[22]

In Southport, it was impossible for the music scene in Almond's youth not to feel like a bust after the boom of Merseybeat; Liverpool is only sixteen miles away, its surrounding seaside towns swallowed up by the movement then spat out again once the industry's attention moved on.

Ron Ellis, promoter, DJ, long-time Southport resident: Liverpool had an identity of its own, it had its own hit parade, and Southport was absorbed into that. The Beatles would play the Queen's Hotel, all the other bands making their names would come over here first. There were so many bands and work for them all the time, they could easily play six times a week, until it faded. Even in places where there would be ballroom dancing, at ten o'clock it would switch over to a DJ playing Merseybeat records until two in the morning. It was a very vibrant scene. But by 1967 it had lost the charm. There were still groups coming from Liverpool, but attention had turned elsewhere.[23]

Soft Cell's seaside was not one in which serious decline had set in – that would come through the 1980s and

1990s – but the paint had begun to peel. Every now and then a darkness would emerge beneath the veneer.

Huw Feather: Because Southport had been quite a nice, middle-class, almost posh town to 'take the waters' in the Edwardian period and in the 1920s, it became a place for ill people to either recuperate or die. It's always had that ghost-like presence of all those people who had passed through the town.

Marc Almond: At Southport Fair I had watched an elderly man climb on to the waltzer. When it came to a halt he was slumped, lifeless in one of those semi-circular chairs. He had died of a heart attack.[24]

Once the holidaymakers left, all the opulence that had been constructed to serve their escapist fantasies began to fade. From September, the Blackpool Illuminations would shine against the gathering darkness of winter, but when they were switched off at the beginning of the new year and the pantomimes closed up shop, the bleakness was left stark and unadorned.

Norman Barrett: The circus only used to run until the end of the illuminations, then when the illuminations closed, every-thing in Blackpool closed with them.

If seaside towns are like another world, then those worlds are like planets that spin on a more extreme axis, where the changes in season are more dramatic and pronounced. It is that sense of contrast, between the on- and off-season, the release of seaside entertainment and the emptiness left behind, that would prove most influential on a band for whom the focus was not only the extravagance of the night but also the melancholy of the morning after. As natives of the edgeland, Soft Cell embraced the winters as much as the summers.

Huw Feather: I come from a town with a fairground that closes for six months of the year. That became a fascinating place to visit both during and out of season; in fact, it was even more interesting out of season. In spring I'd watch them paint the new art, the cartoons and the uber-popped-up Victoriana with metallics and bright psychedelic colouring.

Dave Ball: I still love seaside towns when they're out of season. If you live by the seaside, it's nice when there's no tourists around, you can walk along the beach and it's empty and grey. Then a sadness when the fun's over, when the funfair's closed. I always liked to walk around the funfair when it was shut, take my dog out for a walk on the Pleasure Beach when all the rides closed for the winter. That seaside melancholy rubbed off on Marc and me, the atmosphere of that. It's a very northern thing, I think. A dour northern-ness. There's a transience to the neon lights and the candyfloss.[25]

Chapter 2
THE YORKSHIRE VORTEX

In another northern town – the one where the concept of the seaside resort had been born, in fact – for two weeks every summer from 1955 to 1957 a group of radical-thinking artists hosted the Scarborough Summer School. Mostly attended by secondary-school teachers, it was led by the artists and married couple Victor and Wendy Pasmore, and Leeds College of Art tutors Harry Thubron and Tom Hudson, all of whom were among the pioneers of a radical new method of teaching known as Basic Design. Drawing on the revolutionary ideas of the German Bauhaus movement a generation before them, they rejected the constrictive old view that creativity could be taught through formalised systems of movements and disciplines, and instead prized intuitiveness, cross-disciplinary experimentation and a lack of restriction.[1]

As the Basic Design movement spread across Britain's art schools, different tutors brought different variations.[2] Thubron and Hudson's, which they called Basic Research, was among the most influential. Under Thubron's stewardship as Head of Fine Art, Leeds College of Art became defined by anti-authoritarianism and iconoclasm, a rejection of the idea that students should mimic the 'great' artists who had come before them, and an encouragement to embrace the raw creative process itself.[3]

Patrick Heron, painter, writing in the *Guardian*, 1971: [Leeds is] the most influential [art school] in Europe since the Bauhaus, thanks, among others, to Harry Thubron.[4]

Through the 1960s the painter Robin Page, who succeeded Thubron, kept the experimental spirit of Leeds alive, bringing in the likes of his fellow Fluxus artist Yoko Ono and conceptual artist and avant-garde musician George Brecht to lecture. At the end of the decade, Leeds College of Art, now well established as Britain's foremost destination for an avant-garde education, was incorporated into Leeds Polytechnic following the findings of the Coldstream Report of 1960, which argued for the integration of art schools into mainstream education.[5] There were fears from some that the move might dilute that radicalism, but in fact the arrival of national funding to a school like Leeds would lead to a boom.[6]

Geoff Teasdale, Head of School of Contemporary Fine Art Practice, Leeds Polytechnic, 1970–2008: Up until the 1960s, art schools were by and large small institutions, funded by local authorities. Following the findings of the Coldstream Report, the programme at Leeds was now being funded by the Higher Education Funding Council, housed in newly built accommodation, and equipped with space and facilities.[7]

The recruitment of younger practising artists as staff was influential too, and included performance artists such as Robin Page, John Fox of the collective Welfare State and John Darling, who was interested in sound-based performance and built a small studio alongside the area dedicated to performance. Most important of them all was the charismatic anarchist, multi-disciplinary artist, jazz musician – and now lecturer in fine art – Jeff Nuttall, who took to referring to the prevalence of avant-garde thinking in Leeds and surrounding areas as 'The Yorkshire Vortex'.[8]

James Charnley, Jeff Nuttall's biographer and former student: We students were guinea pigs in this experiment in art education. Leeds was a place where you could more or less do what the hell you wanted. Jeff Nuttall fitted right in because he had that anarchic streak. It was the environment where he could do what he did best.[9]

Nuttall's book *Bomb Culture* had been published three years prior to his arrival in 1971. Half sparsely fact-checked document of post-war counterculture, half breathless polemic, it argued that under the spectre of nuclear annihilation that emerged at the end of the Second World War, artists across disciplines and styles should be compelled to react with new-found radicalism. Nuttall saw it in the hyper-charging of jazz music through Charlie Parker's pioneering bebop style, the orgiastic riots that greeted concerts by Elvis Presley and the Beatles, the emergence of teen subcultures like Teddy Boys, mods and rockers that wrought tabloid scandal through their deviation from societal norms, the rise of the Campaign for Nuclear

Disarmament and the politically charged folk music of Bob Dylan and Joan Baez, the centring of the American Anarchist movement around Bernard Marszalek's Chicago bookstore, the surrealist humour of Spike Milligan and *The Goon Show*, the unflinching imagery of Francis Bacon's figurative paintings, the famous beatnik gathering at the Royal Albert Hall in 1965 and more.[10]

Jeff Nuttall, in *Bomb Culture*: [Art] has seldom been closer to its violent and orgiastic roots. What has happened is that the pressure of restriction preceding nuclear suicide has precipitated a biological reflex compelling the leftist element in the young middle class to join with the delinquent element in the young working class for the re-affirmation of life by orgy and violence. What is happening is an evolutionary convulsion rather than a reformation. Young people are not correcting society. They are regurgitating it.[11]

James Charnley: [Nuttall] was at the beginning of the counterculture. To some extent he was its midwife. He saw that if we were all going to die in a nuclear explosion then our fundamental mindset should be altered, that we would become less tied to a militaristic five-day week and open up to a free-loving sort of lifestyle. He was the man when he rocked up in Leeds. Everyone was mightily impressed that he was there.

Under Nuttall and Head of Art Geoff Teasdale, two cultures sprang up in tandem – a combination of Basic Design with that countercultural outlook that promoted self-sufficiency in the students, and a not-unrelated freeing up of time for the teaching staff to get drunk.

Anne Tilby, Leeds Polytechnic student: You had a lot of freedom; you could use different machinery and techniques, have access to materials from different departments. It wasn't structured like other art schools. Consequently, I think the lecturers were in the pub quite a lot.[12]

Ron Geesin, sound artist and visiting lecturer: Certain staff at Leeds took the particularly radical stance of drinking plenty of beer at lunchtime, provoking students with impossible ideas in the afternoon and taking more beer in the evening.[13]

A larger-than-life and highly charismatic *bon vivant*, prone to heavy drinking, abrasive trumpet solos while students were working, unprovoked displays of nudity and numerous sexual dalliances, Nuttall dominated the department, though he was not Head of Fine Art. He remains a controversial figure, remembered by some with admiration, by some in complicated terms, and by others as predatory and a pervert.

Sophie Parkin, artist, writer and Leeds Polytechnic student: I think Jeff Nuttall was both an inspiring person and a terrifying person. He was definitely predatory, but if you got a job in an art school back then, you were a predatory male. Jeff Nuttall was a friend of my stepfather, who also taught there, and they used to boast that they would never spend a night alone because they were always sleeping with one student or another.[14]

James Charnley: Jeff's interest in sex was pretty intense. He tried practically everything, including golden showers, which was information he would share offhand with his students.

Anne Tilby: I think he did pull his trousers down a couple of times to flash his bottom; he was an exhibitionist, but that was just him. I don't think it was out of order, you just couldn't take him seriously. He was great because he'd come in and just argue. If you got intellectual or pretentious, he'd call you out. He could be quite aggressive! I remember thinking he was really scary at first and then just thinking, 'Oh, he's quite hilarious.'

Sophie Parkin: The corridors at the poly were all built with these narrow walls in order to have large studios. I remember Jeff once pinning Marc to the wall like a fly, caught by this rapacious man with his great big stomach.

Dave Ball: He was terrifying. I think as long as you didn't show fear you were OK though. Like if a dog comes up and barks at you – if you let it know you're scared, it'll bite you. When I did my interview to get in, it was Jeff Nuttall and Geoff Teasdale who interviewed me. They were scary, but I took it in my stride.[15]

It was Nuttall and Teasdale who interviewed Almond, too, after his application in 1976. By Almond's own admission, his portfolio was not strong, but the two zeroed in on the nineteen-year-old's nascent ability for performance.

Marc Almond: Jeff was an amazing inspiration to me. He'd make fun of me, but without him I would never have got in. At school I think I had many learning difficulties which are given names now, but which then make you appear stupid, so I went along, and Jeff asked me to do some little performance, and it was him who recommended me for a grant, and I owe him a lot.[16]

When Almond arrived at Leeds as a student the following September, it was Nuttall who had to be his tutor. He – and Dave Ball, who arrived one year after him – became part of a student cohort where there was a culture of one-upmanship, of pushing things to their extremes.

James Charnley: To a certain extent everyone wanted to please Jeff, so everyone was always trying to outdo everyone else. Nobody wanted to be dull. A lot of people found it psychologically quite difficult because he would push people, so their strengths and weaknesses were exposed. And so, it was something of a psychodrama.

Marc Almond: The more extreme, shocking, visceral, and disturbing a performance was, the more he applauded and enthused.[17]

At one now infamous performance called *Senseless*, two students named Derek Wain and Peter Parkin had invited an unsuspecting audience of about one hundred students and staff into a black-painted room and locked the doors. The stage lights rose gradually to reveal cathode ray televisions, bowls of goldfish and a number of budgies and white mice tethered to tables with fishing wire around their legs. The song 'Camptown Races' was played over a PA as the two artists emerged wielding air rifles, breaking the bowls to leave the fish flapping on the floor, and smashing the television screens to get the birds to start flapping. As it became apparent that they intended to shoot the defenceless animals a riot broke out which ground the show to a chaotic halt. Accounts vary as to whether Wain and Parkin were actually able to kill any of the animals.[18]

Peter Parkin, speaking to the *Daily Telegraph*, 17 November 1976: One of the audience threw a TV set at me and then started hitting us with an iron bar we had from breaking the sets. I tried to shoot one of the budgies but blood was pouring down my face and I didn't have my sights on so I couldn't have hit it.[19]

Geoff Teasdale: It was known at the time as 'The murder of the budgies'. Although Leeds had become notable as a centre for performance art with many students taking up the opportunity in a responsible and professional manner, this incident was singularly an exception. It's important to record that no animals were injured since the event was stopped by the intervention of the audience!

The performance was envisaged as a comment on the violence of modern life, but people were so incensed that, two weeks later, Wain and Parkin were seriously assaulted and beaten up. They were also charged by the police with 'ill-treating and causing unnecessary suffering' to the animals and fined £20 each. Nuttall, who had directly inspired the piece, spoke on the students' behalf at their trial.

Jeff Nuttall, as reported in the *Daily Telegraph*, 27 May 1977: Obviously when you are presenting an imaginative piece an element of surprise is very important. I believe it was the intention of the students in their conscious minds to represent something which would reveal a lack of affection or sympathy, of compassion which is prevalent in society.[20]

Derek Wain, as reported in the *Daily Telegraph*, 27 May 1977: Art to me is an expression of my environment. If I portray a grisly image then you have only society to blame.[21]

Although never managing to scandalise to quite the same extent as *Senseless*, Almond took plenty of Nuttall's anarchic, provocative spirit into his own practice. For the next forty-five years and counting, in fact, it would never leave him. Additional inspiration was to be found in his immediate surroundings. One night, trying to sleep in his damp bedsit in the run-down area of Chapeltown, a police raid revealed that the clomping footsteps he would hear upstairs every night were in fact the sound of customers entering an illicit brothel. He began writing poetry and sketching out stage designs as he developed an intense – but always blackly comic – style. He began producing Super 8 films, too.

Marc Almond: My first half-hour epic, entitled *Glamour in Squalor*, featured drag queens and punks committing acts of violence in filthy bedsits. *Teenage Vice* featured a girl and a boy – both punks – observed through a crack in the door as she provoked him into an argument. Eventually he killed her with a red silk cord and scrawled the words 'Teenage Vice' across her naked back in red lipstick. No marks from the feminists for that one! Another was about a shadowy figure living in a squalid bedsit. The camera explored the room, the ornaments and the objects contained within, eventually alighting on a figure dressed in grey and sitting on an old sofa. The figure was eating a can of cat food, then picked up a book and started to thumb through it, looking at photos of yesteryear. The photos flickered to life, and bizarre-costumed people danced across the pages.[22]

Early performances – where the films were also screened – included *Icebox*, where Almond sat in front of a mirror, naked except for black boots and a swastika covering his penis, shaved half his body, covered half of his face in garish makeup, smashed the mirror and cut himself with a shard before simulating sex. Another was a cabaret based on the anonymous Japanese poem *The Vampire Cat of Nabéshima*, about a demonic feline who kills a princess and assumes her shape in order to drain blood from a prince, for which Almond enlisted help from his Southport friend Huw Feather – now studying theatre design in Nottingham – and fellow student Anne Tilby.

Anne Tilby: I remember wearing lots of bits of leopard fur, and masks that I think were casts of Marc's own face. It was highly decorated papier mâché. I'm sure he was influenced by the decadent imagery and the tackiness of Fellini and Pasolini films – I used to live next door to the Hyde Park Cinema, which would screen them all night, as well as all-night German expressionism.

Huw Feather: I used to travel up a lot on the weekends, because if Marc was putting on a show, he'd involve me in putting it on, figuring out how it should look, asking me whether I'd be in it. Marc would come down to see my shows in Nottingham too, where I had become involved with a big theatre company. I was already designing stuff for the Edinburgh Festival by my second year. I had many, many shows under my belt, so when Marc needed a hand, I would go up and help. His shows at that time were very 'fine art Leeds shows', a full-on assault of the senses, all done within black surrounding spaces, painted blocks and scenery. Oh, and lyrics, too.

The art of inter-war Germany had had a particular effect on Almond. The silent films of Fritz Lang, Karlheinz Martin and Robert Wiene – the directors' emphasis on dramatic contrasts between light and dark, and their worlds' distorted and nightmarish surroundings – chimed with his own desire to seek out the darker sides of Leeds. In Georg Grosz's dramatic caricatures of Weimar socialites he found figures not unlike those he found in Southport's debauched theatre parties. Feather, notably, would stage an ambitious production of the Weimar-set musical *Cabaret* as his degree show down in Nottingham.

Huw Feather: Bob Fosse [choreographer-director of the 1972 film adaptation of *Cabaret*] had predicted what all the smart people would be into by the end of the decade. My production didn't have the budget to cope with all the costume changes. The chorus girls had the correct costumes, and for everything else we just used lingerie – a bit more akin to *Rocky Horror*. It had the historic element, and the nightmare camp but a bit more goth and a bit more in your face. That was the start of my understanding that not everything needed that sugar-pink gilding to make it camp.

Almond and Tilby, meanwhile, formed part of an informal collective, performing in one another's shows, sewing each other's costumes and painting each other's sets. When Tilby presented surreal parody game shows in which participants would have to, for example, make a wig out of bangers and mash, Almond would act as MC. One key figure of the group would be Frank Tovey – later to have a pioneering electronic music career of his own as Fad Gadget.

Anne Tilby: [Tovey] would train us up, make us do exercise classes and run around the park with him. He was influenced by Lindsay Kemp and had been to his classes; I remember him trying to teach us to mime and it was hilarious. I was crap!

Dave Ball: I think Marc was definitely influenced by Frank's Fad Gadget gigs, the way he'd leap around quite manically, taking performance art into a weird underground pop music scenario. I think Marc saw what he could do performance-wise with electronic music.[23]

It was a collective that soon crossed the boundaries between students at the polytechnic and those at the supposedly more prestigious University of Leeds, as well as those between students and ex-students, and between art students and those studying something more 'straight'.

Hugo Burnham, University of Leeds student and Gang of Four drummer: The two campuses were right next door to each other. The university was much older and the polytechnic was supposedly the lesser educational establishment, but that wasn't really borne out by the work people were doing. I went up having grown up in the south, a middle-class public schoolboy and a rugby player, but after about three or four weeks hanging out with the rugby crowd, engineers and medical students, I drifted towards a group of people who looked more interesting.[24]

Annie Hogan, University of Leeds student: I was doing international history and politics at the University of Leeds, the 'red brick university', which all felt very Tory. I couldn't really wait to get out of there. I was mainly in the Faversham pub where there was a brilliant jukebox and a Leigh Bowery lookalike barman. Marc and Dave were there quite a lot too.[25]

Hugo Burnham: They were definitely weirder down at the poly, and it was down there that I found people who knew who Lindsay Kemp was. One of my best friends became Frank Tovey. He was Gang of Four's first roadie! There was a lot of sharing of spaces for rehearsing, sharing of instruments. There were little groups who lasted just one or two shows. We had a heavy metal band called Iron Cross that lasted one show before we realised it wasn't a good idea. There was a lot of mutual support, whether or not you actually liked the work. You'd support them because they were your roommates, or because they were in the same class as your girlfriend. We were all trying do something interesting, whether it lasted five minutes, five months or five years. We would take paintings and make performances out of them like Kandinsky's *The Yellow Sound*. We did *King Lear* with five people in an hour and ten minutes, kabuki style, and toured that around Ireland in the summer.

Then there was Marc. There was only one specific show we did together, part of an adaptation of *From Morning to Midnight*, the Georg Kaiser expressionist piece from 1912, that was being done by the master's programme in theatre direction. Part of the play was supposed to be a cabaret, so the director said they would bring all the audience down to the rehearsal space downstairs where we could put one on – which was a red rag to a bull for me. We served drinks, made the whole room that sort of vibe, then did twenty minutes stolen from the actual *Cabaret* musical. I played the MC, Marc was one of the chorus girls.

The performance of Almond's that would have the most lasting effect, meanwhile, would be *Zazou*. It concerned an androgynous nightclub singer (Almond) in a club called Blue Heaven, his night-time excesses and his nihilistic relationship with a sex worker called Johnny (Tilby).

Marc Almond: The *Yorkshire Evening Post* came to review it, and called it 'one of the most nihilistic, depressing pieces that I have ever had the misfortune to see'. So it was a success then.[26]

Like Almond's cabaret performance with Burnham and his Super 8 films about bedsitters, sleaze and squalor, *Zazou* would prove prophetic when it comes to the themes that would later permeate Soft Cell's work. Perhaps the most notable thing of all, however, was its soundtrack. At one point, Almond's club singer performed a strange electro-disco version of 'Sixteen Going on Seventeen' from *The Sound of Music*.

Hugo Burnham: It wasn't so much songs as performance art with noise.

Friend and collaborator Ed King played guitar, while on synthesisers and Stylophone was another student named Dave Ball. Almond would in fact be the first person Ball spoke to on enrolment day.

Dave Ball: When I arrived, everyone was wearing box-fresh Doc Martens, Wrangler jean jackets. Then, I spot this guy in gold lamé trousers, a black leopard-skin top and dyed black hair. I thought, 'You've got to be in the art department,' so I went up to him and said, 'Where do I enrol?'[27]

The tutor Ball was most drawn to at Leeds was John Darling. Like Nuttall, Darling had been a founding member of the People Show collective, and later joined the avant-garde touring company John Bull Puncture Repair Kit.[28] At Leeds he set up a small recording lab next to the art department, installing reel-to-reel tape recorders, a six-channel line mixer, a turntable, a microphone and an array of sound-effect records. Egg boxes lined the walls and ceiling for rudimentary soundproofing. He named it Radio Hessian, and played a jingle to students as they entered, welcoming them to 'The station with the dark brown sound'.

Dave Ball: It was very homemade, a ham radio sort of place, but I loved it in there. Jeff Nuttall and Geoff Teasdale would be in the pub from eleven 'til three, but John wasn't a big pisshead like that – although he did smoke a bit of home-grown. He was very charming and lovely, he'd do all these mad voiceovers and tape them, and he had a fantastic col-lection of sound-effect records that he'd use to put together all these Pythonesque montages. I used to spend as much time in there as possible. I had placed myself right next to the sound studios so I could see the comings and goings and get to know John a bit. At first, I just had my Fender Telecaster, so I started trying to be like Vini Reilly from Durutti Column with tape delays and guitars.[29]

After Frank Tovey became enraged at Ball's constant 'bor-rowing' of his synthesiser, Ball pawned his guitar in order to buy one of his own. An act of obvious symbolism, Ball was not the only young musician trading in guitars for synths as punk's DIY spirit coincided serendipitously with the instruments' increasing affordability.

Following a number of cultural landmarks – the success of Wendy Carlos's *Switched-On Bach* in 1968 and her soundtrack to Stanley Kubrick's *A Clockwork Orange* three years later, and the BBC Radiophonic Workshop's deployment of groundbreaking electronic production for television and radio soundtracks, for instance – synths had already started colouring mainstream rock music through the likes of Brian Eno's sound treatments for Roxy Music and David Bowie.[30] Now, however, purely electronic pop bands were beginning to emerge. By 1979, synths were prevalent enough that Gary Numan's number-one hits 'Are "Friends" Electric?' and 'Cars' could dominate the British airwaves, and in 1980, Telex's deliberately inane synthpop song 'Euro-Vision' would be Belgium's entry to the song contest of the same name.

Dave Ball: When I traded in my guitar for a synthesiser, John Darling was very excited by the prospect so he was very helpful, messing around with noise and putting sounds together. He was completely bonkers though. He'd once been doing a performance, then decided to drive his van into the Russian embassy because of a weird impulse. After he got arrested, they realised he wasn't quite right in the head, and he was on a lot of medication.[31]

One day, Almond was walking past Radio Hessian and heard the strange noises emanating from inside, Darling's egg-box soundproofing evidently proving ineffective.

Shortly afterwards he asked Ball whether Ball might provide a backdrop for his performances. The two made a curious pairing in both personality and appearance. Ball was tall and broad, thoughtful and introverted, often seen in a tie in an attempt to mimic his heroes Kraftwerk on the cover of their 1978 album *The Man-Machine*. Almond was slight in stature, ostentatious in dress and provocative in nature.

Anne Tilby: Dave was manly. He'd go to the pub, drink beer and at first would ask why he would want to hang around with someone like Marc. But I would say, 'You've got so much in common! If you got over the fact that he's different, you'd get on like a house on fire!'

One such thing they had in common was their taste in music. Both loved the band Suicide, the forward-thinking New York synth punk duo whose trailblazing work forged a path they thought they might follow, as well as Throbbing Gristle. A band with their own roots in provocative performance art, Throbbing Gristle had emerged out of the COUM Transmissions group, whose live shows shocked and awed with the use of self-mutilation, dead animals, nudity and bodily fluids. Throbbing Gristle's debut gig was on the same night as COUM Transmissions' last, at the opening night of their retrospective exhibition *Prostitution* at London's Institute of Contemporary Arts in 1976. With the traditional director's speech substituted for a stripper, glasses of wine replaced by pints of beer, a band called LSD (an early form of what would later be formative punk outfit Chelsea) employed to drown out any sounds of networking, and a false rumour purposely spread that the finale was to see Billy Idol hanged with cheese wire, it provoked tabloid outrage and even a debate in Parliament on the merits of providing public funding for the arts.[32]

Conservative MP Nicholas Fairbairn, speaking to the *Daily Mail*, 1976: Public money is being wasted here to destroy the morality of our society. These people are the wreckers of civilisation. They want to advance decadence.[33]

In their live performances, Throbbing Gristle combined disturbing imagery – hardcore pornography or photographs from Nazi death camps, for instance – with highly distorted music augmented with tape samples and special effects alongside Cosey Fanni Tutti and Genesis P-Orridge's cold spoken-word vocals. Their first album, 1977's *The Second Annual Report*, consisted half of recordings from their live shows (including one based around a recording of an interview with a Canadian murderer) and half of a film soundtrack that had been composed before the film itself. For Almond and Ball, it was to be a model, and just a few years later P-Orridge would become a collaborator.

As well as contributing to *Zazou*, Ball would play an important part in Almond's degree show *Twilights and Lowlifes*. By then, their experiments had gradually morphed into something more structured. On his own, Ball had been writing three-minute pop songs, catchier tracks with actual hooks based around simple disco beats, and Almond liked the way they sounded. Combining them with his poetry seemed an obvious idea, so their experiments began to mutate into more straightforward songs.

Band names like 'Man Made Fibres', 'Here's Health', 'Hard Cell' and 'Soft Soap' were considered, until they landed at last on Soft Cell.

At the Polytechnic's Christmas party on 23 December 1979, Soft Cell performed their debut gig proper as the first act on a six-band bill. Caked in makeup, black satin and Lurex, they made a marked contrast from their combat jacket and jeans-clad bill mates as they began with an early track called 'Bleak Is My Favourite Cliché'. Ball unspooled a spartan and straightforward electro-punk beat, Almond launched into an icy critique of po-faced minimalists.

Marc Almond: The show was shambolic, to say the least. I yelped rather than sang, inspired by very early Siouxsie and the Banshees if anyone – we certainly saw some of our own songs as inhabiting that same dark world. But we ended our set with a song more akin to Throbbing Gristle and Suicide's 'Frankie Teardrop'. It was called 'Persuasion'. Unnerving, it was extremely draining to perform. As the strobe lights flashed, the screen images flickered to a climax, and me screaming through echo effects until the sound became ear-piercing. Then ... silence.[34]

Operating within a city midway through a period of overhaul as its crumbling old neighbourhoods were demolished to make way for newbuilds, the art students and bands took advantage of what remained. In old workers' cottages they found cheap housing. Some of the terraced houses that had been emptied ahead of their planned demolition still had power, so they were commandeered for band rehearsals and parties. Situated almost exactly in the middle of the short walk between the two universities' respective campuses, the Fenton pub became the epicentre of the music scene.

Dave Ball: All the bands used to hang out there. There was no malice, but the Mekons, Gang of Four and Delta 5 all used to sneer at us. They thought we were a novelty joke act, something from the end of the pier; they couldn't understand it. Later, the record companies couldn't get their heads around it either. There had been Sparks and Suicide in America, but there hadn't been a British synth duo before. The public would get it straight away, but the record companies, in this time of supposedly radical punk bands, they didn't get it at all. 'This stupid little synth duo', the other bands used to laugh at us. 'Where are your guitars? Where are your drums?' Well, we said, 'We'll show you we don't need them!'[35]

Hugo Burnham: I'll be honest and say there was a certain degree of jealousy. It was like, 'Soft Cell, fucking hell, just listen to that! And he still can't sing in tune!'

Further afield, the F Club became pivotal, a regular night that would host the most exciting bands in the country and beyond – with the Leeds student cohort often invited to fill support slots.

John Keenan, F Club co-founder: Graham Cardy and I had started putting on bands in the poly common room in the summer of 1977, then when summer finished they wanted the room back and chucked us out. We had a good little crowd of all different kinds of creative people, and I wanted to keep them all together, so I started the F Club. The 'F' stood for 'F' the poly, basically. I put out a flyer that said, 'Let's get the F out of here'. We moved into the Ace of Clubs until Christmas, had people like Siouxsie and the Banshees and Wilko Johnson. The Mekons and Gang of Four also started off there. Then there was … a 'suspicious' fire, and the insurance never paid up. I moved into Roots in Chapeltown, the cosmopolitan area of Leeds, where we had loads of seminal post-punk bands like Joy Division, Magazine, Suicide, and finally in 1978 we moved to the cellar club of Brannigan's in the centre of town.

Marc Almond used to come down and ask if he could help with the gear; he got into a few gigs for free like that, as did a few of the others. I booked Soft Cell to support Split Enz – who later became Crowded House. I remember Marc came to me in a bit of a tantrum, saying 'We've got to put our screen up, but Split Enz won't move their drum kit!' Nobody had even heard of Soft Cell at the time. He knew what he wanted, and he had this kind of attitude that I suppose got him everywhere![36]

Josephine Warden, Soft Cell backing singer as part of Vicious Pink: Leeds was buzzing in the late 1970s. Johnny Thunders and the Heartbreakers, the Sex Pistols, Talking Heads, Suicide, I saw them all. There was so much going on. Enjoying all this was a crowd of people that was always at the same places. Marc and I were two of those faces in that crowd. We just clicked. I think we clicked because we were both a bit different from the norm – well, that's what attracted me to him; he was fabulously, outrageously, madly different and stood out wherever he went. He shone. I liked that.[37]

Dave Ball: It was a really fantastic scene. We were feeding off that and we wanted to be a part of it. I wouldn't go a day without seeing some sort of band. Art college was anarchic, we would do whatever the hell we liked in the day, then go and watch Throbbing Gristle in the evening. They were fantastic days and had a profound impact on how we presented ourselves.[38]

The F Club was, in many ways, simply the Leeds incarnation of a wider cultural evolution taking place across the north of England.

John Keenan: I was pretty much doing the same as Tony Wilson in Manchester and Roger Eagle and Pete Fulwell in Liverpool. They were just bigger music cities.

For Almond, however, there was something more transgressive to be found by delving further into the obscurer corners of the Leeds nightlife. He became a regular at a gay club called Charlie's, hidden on the upper floors of an otherwise anonymous building. When you knocked on the door a hatch would slide back. Entry would be permitted following thorough interrogation. Beyond that was a chequered dance floor in the style of *Saturday Night Fever*, and a clientele drawn primarily from Leeds's community of sex workers.

Chris Neate, Leeds Polytechnic student: There was a shop on the ground floor and offices on the first, so you went up this narrow staircase up to the second floor and knocked on the door where there was this little tiny club. I remember it only being about twenty foot long and twelve foot wide, with a little bar in the corner.[39]

Anne Tilby: We used to like going to the gay clubs, because no one ever bothered you.

In Charlie's they played disco songs, one of which would be as transformative as any other piece of music when it came to shaping Soft Cell: Donna Summer's 'I Feel Love'.

Marc Almond: This song came over the PA in a discotheque, and I had never ever heard anything like this before. It was a great mix of the robotic sound of Giorgio Moroder's electronic music with the emotive heartfelt vocal of Donna Summer. And this cold sound with this warm sound was very inspiring to Soft Cell. It was life changing.[40]

By 1980 Almond was no longer a student. Ball, a year below him, was still studying. To make ends meet, he took two jobs. By day he would work behind the bar at the Leeds Playhouse, and by night he was a cloakroom attendant at the Warehouse, a venue opened by American entrepreneur Mike Wiand in 1979. Having sold the two branches of his hamburger joint, the Damn Yankee, the year prior, Wiand was then informed by an architectural company he had worked with, Bulldog Design (later to plan the Haçienda in Manchester), that a warehouse being used for storage by a funeral company was earmarked for demolition. The plan was to make space for an office building,[41] but Wiand convinced Leeds City Council to let him take on a lease instead. He cleared out the caskets and headstones to make room for what he at first intended to be a Hard Rock Cafe-inspired restaurant.

Dino Wiand, Mike Wiand's son: He wanted waiters on roller skates and trapeze artists, and a massive sound system. While he was searching out the sound system he visited New York, Paris and Marbella – a much more glamorous place back then – and started noticing how big the disco scene was. After that, he decided to have the Warehouse be a restaurant by day and a nightclub by night.

The sound system was so expensive and took so long to make in the south of France, his accountant kept on stealing his chequebook and telling him it could never be paid for and made no sense financially. But Mike was in no way a businessman, he just enjoyed making something amazing and the cost was not even considered. He believed that if you settle for mediocrity, you will fail, and that the other businessmen who owned clubs in Leeds, including Peter Stringfellow, were more interested in profits than making something legendary.[42]

Wiand was also a secret operative for the American National Security Agency. He had first come to Leeds in 1969 when he was stationed at RAF Menwith Hill near Harrogate, which was being used as a major American spy base.

Dino Wiand: It was common knowledge, not what he was working on there, but put it this way, the Leeds–Harrogate area was the enemy number one of the KGB and the Russian government. Mike had a very large collection of spy equipment stored in the Warehouse safe that the West Yorkshire police would loan from him from time to time. The American government used to rent out all the rooms in a London hotel called the Columbia and my dad practically lived there when not in Leeds, it was all spies and service people.

Annie Hogan: If I think about it now, he did kind of look like all the CIA guys you'd see on the telly.[43]

The Warehouse was an immediate success. For the first year, Wiand's mother – who he brought over from America especially – ran the restaurant, which would feature 'Sunday Brunch' performances by the likes of Sylvester, George McCrae, Sugar Hill Gang and even a surprise set from the Village People.

Dino Wiand: All the bands mostly stayed over in the small village of East Morton near Bingley and would go to the local village shop to get their cigarettes, to the amusement of the locals.

Chris Neate: It was quite an iconic setup really; he had a very good sound system for the time. Initially, the people who went there were trendy. I think they had money – they were certainly not hard up, to put it one way. I think there was an article about them in *Vogue* at some point.

Dino Wiand: On the club's opening night, they turned away thousands of people.

Chris Neate: I worked in the burger place, but I got transferred to the club, and a vacancy came up for someone to work in the cloakroom. I must have mentioned it to Marc because that's how he got the job there.

Ian Dewhirst, Leeds Warehouse DJ: I became the DJ in late 1979, and Marc Almond was the cloakroom boy. We weren't close, but I'd nod to him and he'd nod back to me. He was quite flammable, he wouldn't be afraid to get in arguments with anyone, you'd quite often hear screaming matches down from the cloakroom of him arguing with someone about a coat.[44]

As the disco scene began to fade, however, the Warehouse's fortunes took a turn for the worse. Another regular DJ, Greg James, whose pioneering mixing work Wiand had first seen at London's Embassy Club, had left under a cloud.[45]

Dino Wiand: One night when no one showed up, Greg had a tantrum which led to him throwing the turntables over the balcony of the DJ booth, smashing onto the floor and narrowly missing the few customers in the club. Greg was fired. Mike called upon the staff in a crisis situation to see what musical direction the club should turn to.

Chris Neate: As the disco phase came to an end, I think Mike was at a loose end about what to do. Marc and I suggested that perhaps we should do an alternative night. The agreement was that we would take the door money and he would take the bar money. I used to do the flyers and stuff like that, and at the start I'd stay on the door to decide who could and couldn't come in, whether they looked alright or not. Marc focussed on the DJing. I was terrible at that. I've never been able to manage machinery. We opened an account at Jumbo Records, and we used to look through *NME* for all our leads.

We put flyers up at Jumbo Records, the Fenton, clothes shops like X Clothes and Funny Wonder, and word of mouth got around. People came from quite a wide area because you couldn't really hear the music anywhere else; they weren't just from Leeds – they were coming from places like Batley and Wakefield too. Some people even came over from Manchester and Liverpool because they'd heard about it. Eventually though, Mike wanted to change a lot about how it was run and put us on a wage rather than the door takings, which were probably too big in his eyes.

Ian Dewhirst: Monday nights were great. I was hearing stuff you wouldn't hear anywhere else, lots of the early electro stuff, like 'Empire State Human' by the Human League. There were six or seven hundred people down there, extravagantly made up and wearing next to nothing. It was great! And Marc was at the epicentre of all that.

Chris Neate: We left and started out at another nightclub called Heaven and Hell. At some point we also started a night in Manchester at a place called De Ville's.

There was also Le Phonographique, where DJs such as the influential Claire Shearsby held sway, and Amnesia where Annie Hogan – who was to go on to become one of Almond's closest collaborators – first cut her teeth both behind the decks and as a booker.

Ian Dewhirst: Annie was always hassling me for something like 'Oh Bondage Up Yours!' [by X-Ray Spex], a lot of the punkier stuff. I'd been playing mostly soul, but the crowd was clearly changing, and at Amnesia people were becoming a lot more fashion conscious. I started buying some of the records that Annie was asking for, just to show that I wasn't unhip. Eventually she was getting on my nerves so much that I said, 'Well why don't you do a bit of DJing?'

Annie Hogan: It was a horrible place but I really loved it. A real dive, a dance floor with a big mirrored beam in the middle. It was a great place where everybody was just cool. Boys kissing boys and girls kissing girls.[46]

At the Adelphi pub, Brian Moss – soon to form his own band, Vicious Pink, with Josephine Warden with production from Ball – was one of the local upstarts setting up alternative nights of their own.

Brian Moss, Soft Cell backing singer as part of Vicious Pink: They let us have the room upstairs for free because they'd sell lots of beer. It's not far from the Tetley's brewery so you'd get a lot of real ale drinkers in there. They never caused any trouble because they'd be too busy watching the girls go up the steps in their short skirts and fishnet stockings.[47]

Jumbo Records in the nearby Merrion Centre shopping mall was another meeting point, as were clothing shops and second-hand stalls there and at Kirkgate market; as important as the sound of this emerging subculture was the way its practitioners looked.

Bedsit Land

Brian Moss: At the other pubs and nightclubs you'd have to wear a shirt and tie or a jacket to get in. A friend of mine came from Wakefield to go to the Warehouse in a shirt and tie, and the guy on the door said, 'It's not for you!' He said he was looking through the window and that he could see all these people dressed proper way out. The following week he ditched the shirt and tie.

Dino Wiand: Mike was very aware at the time the Warehouse was opening that there was a lot of fighting in clubs, with the National Front and football hooligans. He wanted a place for the weirdos, the artists, the gay community, to not feel threatened or in danger. He had a very strict door policy that made it very hard for troublemakers and homophobes to get in.

Chris Neate: People were very 'dressy', put it that way. It was all about posing, really – and drinking too, they weren't just standing about like dummies. There was a lot of second-hand stuff and diamante jewellery, makeup for men and women, bleached hair, and a leaning towards sci-fi that was linked to the whole Kraftwerk thing. Punk had had a big effect, the theory of getting second-hand clothes and making a look, pulling together references, but it had merged into New Romantic.

Some people were more creative than others. I used to hang around with a bloke called Lawrence who used to just wear cowboy hats. Roxy – I wouldn't even know what you'd describe him as. He'd make big crowns out of cardboard and have a toilet seat round his neck. It was like a performance, but he wasn't from an artistic background I don't think. He was just like that. They were quite ordinary people, making a big effort to look extraordinary. They were coming from council estates or terraced houses on the outskirts of Leeds, taking the bus looking like some version of Marilyn Monroe or something. It took quite a lot of energy, as well as being brave.

Sophie Parkin: There were very few of us like that, though. I was appalled at the lack of visual attention that most art students were presenting themselves with. This is art school! This is your excuse to dress up as a piece of art every day! The way we dressed wasn't for an audience, so much as it was your own suit of armour. It was our way of signalling to each other, how we were separate from all of those people.

Their flamboyance was both rare and brave. There was already an air of acrimony towards students in a city divided firmly between 'town and gown', not helped by the regular usage of the polytechnic as whipping boy by the press when seeking to portray students as layabouts, leeching off the taxpayer.[48]

Daily Telegraph, 12 March 1976: An inquiry into why a £395 grant was made to three graduates to walk around with a 10ft yellow pole balanced across their heads is being sought by Mr Ken Weetch, Labour MP.[49]

There was also a pervasion of outright homophobia and transphobia that often led to physical harassment and assault. On a train in 1979, for instance, Almond was assaulted by a gang of forty football fans, forced to hide in the driver's compartment until the police could intervene.[50]

Hugo Burnham: If you were downtown late at night, you were always wondering who was out there to put a bottle in your face for being a 'fucking poof'.

Brian Moss: One friend was attacked and got his skull fractured just for having dyed red hair and makeup on.

Annie Hogan: I got slapped by the bloody doorman at the Phono. Walking through the Merrion Centre with your hair bleached and what have you was very scary. But you just got on with it, didn't you?[51]

Brian Moss: We learnt to defend ourselves because there was so much hassle. Not by choice, but walking around looking like that, you had to be able to look after yourselves. I had a night upstairs at the Three Legs, which is where a lot of Leeds United supporters congregated. It went well for a few weeks, but one night all these guys started attacking all the people leaving my event. It ended up being a massive brawl on the dual carriageway, stopping all the traffic, and we ended up getting the upper hand. I think they got a bit of a shock.

The National Front was close to its peak – its profile raised by violent clashes with anti-fascists in the mid-1970s, the far-right party had not yet reached the schisms that would come with the departure of its leader John Tyndall to form the British National Party in 1982. At one point, the F Club was forced to change its name to the Fan Club in order to distance itself from false allegations in the leftist magazine *The Leveller* that the 'F' stood for 'fascist'.

The Yorkshire Vortex

Hugo Burnham: There was one night the Front all came into the Fenton. I walked in and I could tell something was in the air. They were all crowded around the jukebox giving everyone leery looks, playing Tom Robinson's 'Glad to be Gay' over and over again. You just knew it was going to go off, and then there were glasses flying everywhere as we were chasing them out. There was an old lady who used to always stand in the corner of the bar, and she was terrified. It probably felt like the Blitz all over again. A couple of people jumped over to put themselves around her.

For women in particular, in addition to all of this there was also the spectre of the Yorkshire Ripper. Between 1975 and 1980 Peter Sutcliffe murdered thirteen women and attacked eleven more. The first and last of his crimes – and the majority overall – took place in Leeds. Several of his victims were students. Women walked the streets in twos and threes for their safety while an incompetent police force let him slip repeatedly through the net as they chased false leads.[52]

Sophie Parkin: This was the thing that occupied the nation at the time, and we were in the centre of it. It was extremely frightening. And as well as feeling you weren't safe, as a woman you weren't being protected by the men. What we were being told by the students was that women aren't allowed to go out because it's unsafe for them. Not the men, the ones being cruel, heartless bastards. It was, 'Women, you have to hide. You're not even allowed to go into town by yourselves.' I would never have gone up to a policeman to say, 'Would you look after me?' because I didn't trust the police.

Dave Ball: [Sutcliffe] murdered one of the students at the university, that was hideous. It shocked us. The atmosphere in Leeds at that time was incredibly creepy and heavy. Walking down the street, if there was a woman in front of me, I'd deliberately make sure she could hear me walk on the other side of the road. Between that and the shadow of the National Front, it was all pretty grim up north.[53]

Such were Jeff Nuttall's proclivities, that on at least one occasion he was arrested and questioned as a Ripper suspect. At the Warehouse, meanwhile, clubbers were regularly told to stop dancing so the police could play a tape that was suspected to be from the murderer in the hope that someone in attendance might recognise the voice. The so-called 'Wearside Jack' recording would in fact turn out to be a hoax, leading police astray and giving Sutcliffe even more space in which to continue his crimes.

Soft Cell formed in a Leeds buoyed by radicalism and freedom, at the intersection of punk and early electronic music, amid the vitality of a young and diverse artistic community. Yet it was also a community on which darkness encroached from all sides: things more viscerally evil than anything that could have been conjured at art school. With conceding not an option, that community was forced to become stronger in response: more transgressive and outrageous, whether in sounds, images or words. In just a few short years, Soft Cell would be the biggest pop group in the world, but just like the seedy thrills of the seaside before it, both the darkness and the radicalism of Leeds would remain with them through it all.

Chapter 3
MEMORABILIA

Though Soft Cell were to be one of the bands to originate synth pop, they and their contemporaries in Leeds also
can be considered in the lineage of punk. Almond, as well
as many other of the scene's key players including Hugo
Burnham, Josephine Warden and John Keenan, were all
present when the infamous Sex Pistols-led Anarchy tour,
also featuring the Damned (later to be thrown off the tour),
the Clash and Johnny Thunders, came to the polytechnic in
December 1976. It was the first of only three of the tour's
original dates to take place as scheduled, as local councils
across the country banned the Pistols amid a furore of moral
panic following the infamous TV interview with Bill Grundy
on *Today*.[1]

Hugo Burnham: It was full but not packed, I think a lot of
people were scared. There was a lot of 'security', which was
just the filth but not in uniform. You could sense that they
were itching to whip out a cosh and have a go at these 'fucking punks', these 'fucking students'. It was menacing in a way,
but really exciting in another. John Lydon was mesmerising.

A performer you couldn't take your eyes off. You felt like you were at something exciting and groundbreaking. It felt like it gave you a licence to do things your own way. There was one guy in Newcastle running a local pub, probably in his mid-thirties, who had decided he wanted to be down with the punks so he shaved half his beard off and rolled one trouser leg up. Delightfully pathetic, but at least he was doing it!

Anne Tilby: Our work was punk, and it was a backlash towards Thatcherism.

Though a fact, it is a well-worn cliché that the Anarchy tour inspired a whole generation of young creatives who witnessed it, but what is telling is that for those in Leeds, it was punk's theatrical side that most appealed.

Hugo Burnham: We were all already into Dr. Feelgood, and it was that same 'bringing it back to basics' thing, but this was bringing it back to basics with added colour. To us, the Damned were like the *Rocky Horror Picture Show*. Then John Lydon was like something from traditional music hall – he really knew how to wind up a crowd.

Anne Tilby: I had been to see *Rocky Horror* down in London when I was fourteen or fifteen, and looking back I think that was like a founder of punk. Little Nell was like Siouxsie Sioux before Siouxsie Sioux, the sound that came out of her.

Of all the elements of 1970s British punk music to which Soft Cell were indebted, however, it was in fact the strides made by Buzzcocks that would be the most useful: more specifically, their record label New Hormones. Whereas the London bands, for all their supposed radicalism, were backed by major labels eager to cash in on the phenomenon (the Clash by CBS, the Sex Pistols by EMI, at least until they were dropped following the Bill Grundy interview), Buzzcocks were the only major punk band to do things *entirely* on their own terms. In light of the implosion of the Anarchy tour, it seemed to the young band that punk would be over before they had had a chance to get started.

Pete Shelley, Buzzcocks: At that time it looked like the gig was up, that people had found us out and the whole punk thing was just gonna die a death. The impending thought was that this could all be over quite soon. That was the motivating factor. We wanted to make a record just to say, 'This actually existed'.[2]

To minimise costs and maximise their time in the pub afterwards, Buzzcocks spent only an hour or so in the studio with their friend and 'agent', a would-be producer called Martin Hannett, who allowed them access after the 'proper' bands were finished. They borrowed £600 from a coalition of friends, teachers and family members to press one thousand records, the smallest number possible, with the intention of selling some at their gigs.

They did not originate the idea of independent music, of course. In the earlier punk movement, the Chiswick label had been home to Joe Strummer's pre-Clash outfit the 101ers, while Chiswick's competitors Stiff had released arguably the first punk single of all time in the Damned's 'New Rose'. For generations there had been independent outlets that were nimbler than the majors, quicker to react to talent out of left field. Like almost all of the imprints who had preceded them, however, Stiff and Chiswick were being run by figures who already had ties to the music industry. New Hormones represented a radical break not only from the mainstream but from the extant independent labels too. The first ever document of a band doing things entirely on their own terms.

Steve Diggle, Buzzcocks: Before that it was like EMI had some divine, mythical right to print this mysterious black vinyl stuff and no one else was allowed. There was always somebody in town who could make you a table, bake you a loaf of bread or fix your car, but you never knew a bloke down the road who could make you a record.[3]

As well as launching Buzzcocks' career and proving punk was not, in fact, in its death throes, New Hormones would also provide Soft Cell with a model. Despondent that none of the sixty or so demo tapes the band had sent out to the music industry – including one given by hand to Factory Records' Tony Wilson after he delivered a guest lecture at Leeds – had elicited a response, and having not realised that their fellow student Mike Hannett was the brother of the by-now-renowned producer Martin, they, like Buzzcocks before them, borrowed the money from family to press their debut EP *Mutant Moments*.

Dave Ball: My dad had recently died, so my mum had got lots of money. I persuaded her to lend me four hundred quid to get a thousand singles pressed up. We made a label called

Memorabilia

Big Frock Rekords – I think that was a name Huw Feather came up with. We'd sent tapes out, but no one was interested, so we thought we'd just do it ourselves.[4]

In practical terms, the EP was something of a disaster, with three hundred of the thousand sleeves going missing. As an artefact, however, it is an important document, the sound of Soft Cell's strange roots with the layers of glitz and melodrama that were to follow stripped away to reveal the dark heart that would always lie underneath. A version of 'Frustration', later to evolve into the swinging, sax-adorned opener of *Non-Stop Erotic Cabaret*, is here a thumping cut of warped industrial, betraying their love of Throbbing Gristle. The electronics are crude and experimental, the atmosphere cloying and claustrophobic. The EP's artwork reflects the sci-fi, horror films and gothic literature that they were devouring – one track left unrecorded (for now) was 'Martin', based on George A. Romero vampire-slasher of the same name. The front cover, designed by Ball, shows figures with angular oversized heads set in stark monochrome, leering with uncanny grins. The back, designed by Almond, shows the band, including their then visual collaborator Steven Griffith, as freaks of nature, and the question 'Who's your favourite mutant?'

Dave Ball: Steven was another friend from art college. We'd seen the Human League and Cabaret Voltaire, they all seemed to have some sort of visual thing going on, so we thought, 'Why don't we have one?' He was our third member, even though he didn't have anything to do with the music. Eventually he said, 'Look, this is ridiculous, I can't be a member of the band because I'm not playing anything,' and we didn't really need him, so we went our sperate ways. The last I heard he was in New York, married to a very wealthy woman.[5]

By mid-1980, Almond and Ball had graduated with a 2:1 and a 2:2, respectively. Almond had embarked on a disastrous move to Nottingham to stay with Huw Feather and his girlfriend Liz Pugh in 1979, intercut with a brief sojourn to London where he worked on the door of a Soho clip joint (a period later to provide immense wells of inspiration). Ball had spent the following summer saving up money by sweeping the floors and removing dead rats in a wholesale food warehouse in Blackpool, before he was forced to resign after experiencing intense allergic reactions. Both drawn back into the Yorkshire Vortex, they decided that Soft Cell should be their chief concern.

Dave Ball: I didn't really have much going for me in Blackpool other than stacking shelves. I thought, well, I'll go back to Leeds and give Soft Cell a go.[6]

Josephine Warden: Marc was becoming a real sensation around Leeds and the poly because it was known as a great night out! Everybody was invited to dance, collective participation, especially as it got further and further into the set. There was never a divide between audience and band, and Marc is such a good performer, really good at making everyone part of the show, party time for everyone.[7]

Having gained a small local following, Soft Cell gigged as far afield as Manchester and York. Shows were chaotic, occasionally spilling over into violence, not least one night in Bradford when Almond – dressed as 1960s sci-fi puppet Captain Scarlet – was punched in the face by one gig-goer who thought he was dancing too closely with his girlfriend. Here, and on other occasions, Ball and Griffith were as much bodyguards as bandmates.

Almond and Ball were now living together at 27 Leicester Grove, a housing association building consisting of numerous bedsits and a shared living space. Other occupants included Chris Neate, Cyrus Bruton of 4AD-signed band Dance Chapter, and Annie Hogan. It was here that much of Soft Cell's debut album would be written, and that 'Bedsitter' would be written directly about.

Dave Ball: There were six flats and a big kitchen area with a lounge. At first, I was just crashing on the couch because the girl on the top floor was supposed to be moving out. She was in a band called Girls Are Best. It was a bit of a commune. Marc had the job at the Warehouse in the evening and the Playhouse at lunchtime, then I was just signing on. We'd have the odd gig where we'd get paid a few quid and get fed, but we were very, very impoverished at the time. There were lots of mice running around, I used to hear them under me when I was sleeping on the couch. I once managed to behead one when it ran across the work surface when I was slicing some bread. I had a lucky shot. I'm not proud of myself but it was trying to nick my bread. Survival of the fittest! Later in the video for 'Bedsitter' there's a rat in it which is based on exactly that.[8]

Bedsit Land

Chris Neate: It was a bunch of rooms with a washbasin each, then a shared bathroom, kitchen and sitting room. It was a mess. Well, it wasn't a mess when I first moved there, but it became a mess. I had some big old red velvet curtains that I got when the church at the bottom of the road had been closed down. I rescued it from a skip, as well as loads of other religious artefacts. At the end of the street was a little shop, the basement of a house almost, called Taj Stores. He'd split packets so you could buy one egg and one cigarette at a time from him, which is what we used to do.

Annie Hogan: It was absolutely formative. An open-minded kind of place, it was always great fun and we were all pretty fucked all the time. It was wild! We were all mates, and the kitchen was where everybody came together, especially at night and early in the morning. Well, more like lunchtime. There was a lot of music. Dave remembers me just playing John Barry non-stop, and I remember a lot of disco coming from Marc's room. Dave's room was opposite mine, and a lot of sounds were coming out of there. I walked in one time and he had 'Downtown' by Petula Clark on his system, which is the first record I'd ever got when I was three, and he was remixing it. In 1980 that was quite mind-blowing.[9]

Josephine Warden: It was tiny. God knows how it inspired Marc or Dave to do anything.[10]

Though Soft Cell were starting to get paid to perform, it was not much; their first paid show at the Warehouse brought in £40. More important was the food and drink they would sometimes get for free at the venues. Ball would return to

Blackpool once a month to get his washing done, and return with a few pounds of pocket money to spend on bread, margarine and the cheapest cigarettes available. However, their big break would arrive on 13 September 1980.

John Keenan: The Futurama Festival in 1980 was a big event. I'd done the first one in 1979 at the Queen's Hall, all for then-rising bands. The next year I had U2, Echo and the Bunnymen, lesser known but quite hip bands like Young Marble Giants and Robert Fripp's League of Gentlemen. Siouxsie and the Banshees headlined the first night, and Gary Glitter headlined for some light relief on the second.

Annie Hogan: Soft Cell were on early, and it was mind-blowing for me. It really grabbed me. Marc was crazy and Dave was like a menacing bouncer. There had been [two-piece] bands before like Suicide and Sparks, but there was something different about these two. Probably that seaside misery and British northern-ness to it. It had a massive impact on me. I had taken a lot of do-dos, so afterwards I had to get carried back to the flat.[11]

NME, 20 September 1980: Soft Cell were on stage, an electric band I think, although it might have been a loud buzz in the PA. They limped through a version of 'Paranoid'. I went outside for a walk.[12]

Marc Almond, interviewed in Sounds, 21 March 1981: It was the most awful thing I've ever seen, the absolute pits, a swamp. Like an indoor Reading Festival; a constant stream of bands piling on and off the stage. When we were playing there was another band doing their soundcheck![13]

Soft Cell were not the only electronic upstarts on the bill at Futurama Festival. Higher up the bill that day were Clock DVA, who had sprung from the same Sheffield band – the Future – that was to produce the Human League. The following day would see a show from Naked Lunch, a gang of London punks-turned-analogue-synth-enthusiasts appearing as part of their 'Electronic Indoctrination' tour.

Even in guitar world, things were changing. Bowie's work with Brian Eno on *Low* had displayed the possibilities of embracing the Krautrock revolution within pop. Ultravox, then spelling their name with an exclamation mark in tribute to Neu!, went so far as to actually enlist the German scene's most feted producer, Conny Plank, for their transformational 1978 album *Systems of Romance* and its all-conquering follow-up *Vienna*. Though they did not achieve the same levels of lasting fame, Croydon's Neu Electrikk were also among the major innovators.

Steve Parry, Neu Electrikk: When Neu Electrikk formed [in 1978] there was a lot of interest in electronic music following the earlier release of David Bowie's *Low* and Iggy Pop's *The Idiot.* Although not an electronic album, the Velvet Underground's 'banana' album [*The Velvet Underground & Nico*] continued to be a huge influence, with John Cale's droning viola and exciting experimentation. I was also listening to bands like Neu!, Cluster, Can and Tangerine Dream. Jean-Michel Jarre and Isao Tomita's *Snowflakes Are Dancing* were also on my radar. The British musician Bill Nelson embraced electronic technology with his far-reaching experimental sounds, his instrumental track 'Blimps' certainly made a big impression with me. Another huge influence had to be Brian Eno and Robert Fripp.[14]

While Echo and the Bunnymen's use of a drum machine – the titular 'echo' – was proving quietly revolutionary on Merseyside, and Orchestral Manoeuvres in the Dark's aptly titled 'Electricity' made waves underground, it was Gary Numan who would record Britain's first big electronic pop hit. Entering the studio to make an album with his guitar-based punk band Tubeway Army, he stumbled upon a Polymoog synthesiser and rewrote the group's entire catalogue.[15] Number-one single 'Are "Friends" Electric?' arrived the following summer.

Just thirty miles away from the Leeds scene, in Sheffield, Cabaret Voltaire had blazed an early trail for the city's own electronic experimenters, employing tapes and visual back-drops. In their wake the Human League had formed out of their own strange debris of performance art and modu-lar synths – their roots lie variously in a local youth thea-tre group called Meatwhistle, a performance art collective called Musical Vomit, and founders Ian Craig Marsh and Martyn Ware's jobs as computer operators.[16]

Dave Ball: There had been bands before us like the Human League and Fad Gadget who were doing this strange, alien-ated post-punk electronica, and so I suppose that's where we fit in, on the tail end of that.[17]

Steve Parry: In the beginning I wasn't really aware of a 'scene' as such. To be honest I was more interested in establishing Neu Electrikk. We were in a creative bubble and completely immersed in developing our own sound.

The strange sounds the Human League made – as well as those of Orchestral Manoeuvres in the Dark and Numan – had also reached the Basildon bedrooms of a young Depeche Mode, who also took advantage of cheap synthesisers and changed direction in an effort to follow their lead.[18]

Depeche Mode would soon find a home on Mute records. Set up by Daniel Miller, initially in the New Hormones model, Mute was an outlet purely for the release of his own revolutionary synth experiments 'T.V.O.D.' and 'Warm Leatherette', which he released under the name the Normal; the tracks' cult success gave the label a future. Almond and Ball's art-school friend Frank Tovey, who Ball had enraged by 'borrowing' his synthesiser a couple of years earlier, was now recording as Fad Gadget and would be Mute's very first signing.

Daniel Miller, Mute records: Marc had obviously heard that Frank had put out a record on Mute, so he gave him a demo to give to me. I quite liked it. I remember Marc's vocals being very distinctive and operatic, but I thought 'I can't start working with any more artists.' I was overloaded with even one. Wrong place, wrong time, really. If it had come a bit later, it might have been a very different story.[19]

Around this time, one particular subset of young clubgoers were witnessing the growing influence of electronics in pop music in real time.

Darla-Jane Gilroy, Blitz Kid: The Blitz Kids were a very small group. There was maybe a dozen of us that were really part of it, an art school community plus a few waifs and strays who didn't fit in elsewhere.[20]

They were so-called due to their frequenting of the Blitz in Covent Garden's Tuesday club night, which had itself grown out of Rusty Egan and Steve Strange's David Bowie night at another club called Billy's. As well as Bowie, Egan played plenty of Roxy Music, Iggy Pop and Kraftwerk, despite the fact the latter were still seen by many as a curio.

Rusty Egan: At first 'Autobahn' was put in the bracket of 'Popcorn', 'Sparky's Magic Piano', the 'Doctor Who' theme and Chicory Tip.[21]

As the profile of the young electronic musicians inspired by such music kept growing, Egan would slip more and more of their music into his sets too.

Darla-Jane Gilroy: The music Rusty was playing was reflecting our tastes as much as it was shaping it – although he might not like me saying that. Things like Kraftwerk. My God, I think I wore a groove into those records just playing them over and over and over. I think every fashion show I went to was playing it.

Most of the Blitz Kids were students at two nearby art colleges, Saint Martins and Central; here, that spirit of one-upmanship that was also present at the Leeds Warehouse went into overdrive.

Darla-Jane Gilroy: People like to pretend it wasn't competitive, but of course it was; friendly competition, I'd say, but always an air of wanting to outdo each other. It was like the court of Louis XIV – who could have the highest hair? The biggest shoulder pads or the highest heels? There was a revolving process of create, wear out, create, wear out. It was maximum creativity. There were definitely themes – a big ecclesiastical theme was one of them at the time – but it was just about doing our own thing. I remember my big Nefertiti hat, and a bright red Thierry Mugler-type plastic raincoat where the shoulders were so high, they looked like bricks. I made my own shoes, too. People were shouting at me in the street, but I didn't care.

Accusations of snobbery have been levelled at the Blitz, particularly given its legendarily strict dress code enforced by Strange – in a masterstroke of publicity, he once refused entry to Mick Jagger on the grounds of fashion – but the barriers were as much protective as they were elitist. As with Leeds, these were turbulent times for London; the Winter of Discontent and its associated refuse workers' strikes had seen refuse piled high in Leicester Square, just yards from what would later be the Blitz's front door.[22] The insidious rise of violence – much of it racially and sexually motivated – was not confined only to the north.

Sophie Parkin: Everywhere was much more violent in those days, probably because of the trauma from the Second World War. Closing time at the pubs was 11 o'clock, so everybody was out on the streets by quarter past. There were always fights outside of every big pub. If you walked down Ladbroke

Grove or through the West End at half past eleven – which if you were sensible you never did – there'd be massive fights, really violent fights. People being bottled, ambulances being called. And that was normal.

Darla-Jane Gilroy: The club was a safe space, outside was not. We'd drop Stephen Linard [Blitz Kid and fashion designer] off, and he didn't have to walk far to get home, but he'd get stopped maybe four times in the space of forty minutes. It was a completely different experience outside of the club. With punk there had been the birth of places like the 100 Club and the Vortex that created mixed audiences – reggae artists would play, so Black kids would come. The Blitz was a further amplification of that, where you got Black and White, gay and straight, weird and not weird all together.

Strange, acting as the face of the club, and Egan, providing its sound, embodied the two forces that were colliding to create this moment of major cultural import.

Darla-Jane Gilroy: Steve and Rusty complemented each other perfectly. Steve had a genius for creating his image, and the image of people around him. He always saw the potential in other people. If he saw a fashion designer, he'd say, 'Right, I want you to design something for me', and then he'd wear it. The only person who had reinvented himself that much in an exterior way until then was David Bowie. And Rusty, what people often overlook is that he's an incredible musician in his own right.

Music has always had a relationship with fashion, but this is the point at which it became very intensified. One day a guy called Perry Hines came into Saint Martins, threw this fancy thing down on the table and said, 'This is gonna be really big, it's called *i-D.*' So you've got the birth of the style press, the people generating the looks, the stages at the clubs where you can make your presence felt, and you've got the sound of that generation, all coming together at the same time.

Rusty Egan: It was this golden era, this time when people who went to clubs didn't just hold up a phone and wear high-street clothes – they didn't even have a landline! It was 'See you next week', then they'd go to the markets or all-night cinemas, make some clothes and listen to one album three hundred times until they heard something new played by the DJ – me! I had a record shop too, and they all came in on Saturday afternoon. Then I'd tell them about a gig, and I'd put them on the list. It was an amazingly creative time.

Similar scenes were emerging in other cities, particularly in Birmingham where the opening of designers Khan & Bell's Hurst Street shop proved a petri dish of its own.[23] In the press these movements soon became clumsily packaged, their practitioners dubbed Futurists, the Cult with No Name and, most commonly, the New Romantics.

Darla-Jane Gilroy: Once the press got hold of things it started to change. There was some element of, 'Who are these ridiculous kids with their fancy makeup?' I think it started to destroy the atmosphere; people started coming to stand and stare.

Egan and Steve Strange – who had by now also formed an electronic band of their own with Midge Ure in the form

of Visage, partly to provide songs for Egan to DJ with –
moved on to increasingly larger spaces, first the Club For
Heroes on Baker Street, and then again to the Camden
Palace. Other clubs also took up the mantle – Le Beat
Route, located directly underneath Saint Martins, for example. Heaven, London's first large-scale gay club, opened in
1979.

In another Soho bar, the musician Richard Strange (for-
merly of the Doctors of Madness and no relation to Steve)
had founded a club of his own called Cabaret Futura, which
put its focus directly on the embrace of a number of different art forms and the possibilities of their combination – not
unlike the philosophy that had defined the teaching at Leeds
Polytechnic.

Richard Strange, musician, Cabaret Futura founder: I had just
come back from touring America with a tape recorder. In
middle America it had been hard going – I was not neces-
sarily what they wanted to see – but in New York and Los
Angeles there was a lively cross-fertilisation of art. There
were these clubs that had a wider clientele than just rock
music fans; it was more arty. There was this tradition already
there, of cross-fertilisation between painting, graffiti, fashion, music, spoken word. All those bands like Talking Heads,
Blondie, Television and Richard Hell had come out of Andy
Warhol and the Velvet Underground. Those places excited
me more than playing the 100 Club or the Marquee Club
back in London. As much as I had loved those venues back
in the day, it wasn't what I wanted to do any more. So instead,
I thought I'd open my own club, put this mix together myself
and see what happens. I was not someone who'd run clubs

before, I just did it because I wanted to put myself into a different sort of context.[24]

Guardian, 15 January 1981: The multi-media 'cabaret' that Strange put on there has been a mixture of the impressive (mime and songs by Philip Japp [sic] or poems by the Skids' Richard Jobson) and the dreadful (last Sunday's power drill dissection of a dead rabbit by a very noisy 'mime' team from Belfast). Between the acts, Strange plays records of thirties French and German cabaret songs.[25]

A cabaret in the truest sense, Strange's embrace of equality between art forms was not unlike that that was taught at Leeds Polytechnic. Nevertheless, it is the platforming of live bands that remains Cabaret Futura's biggest legacy, not least because Strange would organise the debut London shows of both Depeche Mode and Soft Cell.

Richard Strange: I knew Marc had come out of art school and performance art too. There was that sexual ambiguity with the subject matter of the songs and the way he styled himself. That worked in a cabaret club, you've always got in mind the idea of Berlin in the 1920s and 1930s, the Cabaret Voltaire in Zurich, Dadaism, that frisson of eroticism or sexual ambiguity was very much in the air.

I would be dishonest if I said I could remember every single note they played, but I remember it as being emblematic of a certain moment, a snapshot of the evolution of music. Before then it had been mainly guitars, and now it was going into synthesisers. There were all those bands and they all felt important and exciting. A coming together of creative people from across all disciplines, cross fertilising in an exciting way for a short period of time.

It was to take a figure more singular still to provide the first proper framework for the scene on record, however; a charismatic and anarchic outsider who – when his chaotic course would collide with that of Almond and Ball – would irreparably change not only their lives, but the history of independent music.

Chapter 4
ART TERRORISM

Haverhill-born Stephen Pearce, better known mononymously as Stevo, had spent his adolescence on a number of work placement schemes, first as a painter and decorator, then working in production and manufacturing in Chigwell, and a warehouse in Barking.

Stevo: My father gave me work when I should have been in school. He wanted me to be a carpenter's assistant. Probably the funniest story is hanging up doors in Plumstead. When the wind blew the front door would blow in and stop the pensioners from getting out of the bathroom.[1]

After his mother helped him buy a mobile disco unit on hire purchase, he decided to pay her back through the money he would earn DJing (the unit would later be gifted to Annie Hogan). He performed on Monday nights at the Chelsea Drugstore, then set up at a residency at The Clarendon in Hammersmith. At home he listened to jazz, funk, dance and soul, but the music he played to his audiences was the most intense he could find, embracing the shock and awe of Throbbing Gristle and Cabaret Voltaire.

Then, as throughout his career, Stevo was an outsider. Still in his teens, living with his family in Dagenham, he entered the music industry through sheer force of will, writing 'charts' where he ranked his favourite left-field music and delivering them to *Sounds* magazine.

Beverley Glick, aka *Sounds* magazine journalist Betty Page: At that time, Stevo would handwrite a chart and hand deliver it to the office. He was very good at being proactive – he didn't wait for people. Alan [Lewis, *Sounds* editor] was very keen to make the magazine a broad church; he embraced everything from the New Romantics to the new wave of British heavy metal and everything in between. [Lewis] had an instinct for the zeitgeist and what had the potential to break big. It was a practical thing too – we needed the charts to fill out the page! [Stevo's Futurist] chart became a little mini cult of its own, because he put stuff in there that the more mainstream DJs weren't playing.[2]

Stevo: I was carrying loads of vinyl records up the Kings Road, spinning electronic music and the chart in *Sounds*. I was giving them charts for months on a weekly basis, and it was wonderful to have so much material coming into Dagenham.[3]

Depeche Mode had already signed to Mute after Daniel Miller had seen them perform at one of the shows Stevo promoted at the Bridge House pub in Canning Town, but the artists agreed that their debut release would arrive via a compilation album on Stevo's label Some Bizzare.

Released in early 1981, the *Some Bizzare Album* remains the defining document of that point in British music. It contained not only the nascent megastars – it would also include music from The The and Blancmange alongside Depeche Mode and Soft Cell – but also bands whose lack of mainstream success should not be held against them; Jell's 'I Dare Say It Will Hurt a Little' predates trip hop by decades; the Fast Set's 'King of the Rumbling Spires' is still thrillingly manic; Neu Electrikk's 'Lust of Berlin' a slinky floor-filler.

Steve Parry: After the release of *Some Bizzare Album* I viewed the success of Soft Cell, Depeche Mode, B-Movie and The The with a great deal of pleasure. To see the exposure of the album in the music press and on huge billboards was a real thrill; to have our band up there alongside those hugely respected names gave us great publicity.

Dave Ball: If you look at the bands that were on there, for one eighteen-year-old guy from Dagenham who could hardly read or write, to put together this album and pick out four bands that would get in the proper charts. He could have had a knighthood![4]

After speaking briefly with Almond on the phone, Stevo hitchhiked to Leeds to meet with the band, after which they contributed 'The Girl with the Patent Leather Face' to the album. Recorded in the Leeds Polytechnic studio with John Darling, the song was a transitional one – the halfway point between Soft Cell's scratchy experimentalism and the pounding pop that was to follow.

Stevo: I had placed the [*Mutant Moments*] EP in my chart and I travelled up to Leeds thanks to the band Modern English. They picked me up when I had my thumb out hitchhiking on Staples Corner.[5]

Beverley Glick: There was a dark undercurrent to 'The Girl with the Patent Leather Face' which I had found quite appealing. I liked the Depeche Mode track on the *Some Bizzare Album* too but the Soft Cell track is what I connected with the most. I was going out with [fellow *Sounds* writer] Tony Mitchell, who was very into the emergent fetish scene, and there was a bit of a BDSM vibe about it that I found interesting too.

Stevo also became Soft Cell's manager. While striking a deal between one of his other groups (B-Movie – more conventionally attractive than Soft Cell and better at playing 'proper' instruments) and Phonogram records, he managed to convince the label to sign Soft Cell too, if only as a bonus. The band's relationship with Phonogram was to be uneasy from the very start.

Marc Almond: We were what you would call part of a job lot, a favour granted, and very soon felt unwanted.[6]

He also made sure that Phonogram would send him with a weekly supply of sweets for the duration of Soft Cell's contract, one of many examples of his notoriously unconventional dealings with the music industry. Instead of showing up to meetings, he would sometimes send a stuffed teddy bear by courier, with a tape recorder playing his list of demands. His was a style that injected the chaos of the DIY underground into the corporatised slickness of the mainstream. He took over their well-oiled machinery in service of his self-proclaimed 'art terrorism'.

Dave Ball: He was a proper East Ender – he was for real, and rough around the edges, and I think that energised a lot of people in the music business. He had a residue of punk energy, the DIY mentality, but wasn't just doing it in the bedroom. He used the wheels of industry, used the strike forces of CBS, Phonogram, all to run an indie label.[7]

Stevo had considerable skills when it came to getting challenging music into the mainstream. Just as he had used B-Movie's hype to get Phonogram to take a chance on Soft Cell, he used Soft Cell's success to sell them The The – dropping out at the last minute after playing them off against CBS. He then asked CBS boss Maurice Oberstein to meet him outside Tottenham Court Road tube station at half past eleven at night, Oberstein driving them through the rain to Trafalgar Square. They did not, as was reported, sign the contract atop one of the lion statues, as Oberstein's car was moved on by police after he parked on double yellow lines, but it made a good story that they were all too happy to circulate. As Stevo's larger bands found success, he would use the clout to secure contracts for Cabaret Voltaire at Virgin (Richard Branson's tie, which Stevo is yet to receive, was thrown in as part of the deal) and Genesis P-Orridge's post-Throbbing Gristle group Psychic TV at Warner (with a year's supply of baby food for P-Orridge's child).

Art terrorism

Though the tricks got harder and harder to repeat as time went on – Stevo ran out of luck altogether trying to convince major labels on the merits of Australian-born born musician JG Thirlwell's maniacal 'Scraping Foetus off the Wheel' project (also at times known as 'You've Got Foetus on Your Breath' and simply 'Foetus') in the mid-1980s – Some Bizzare not only had among the most forward-thinking and diverse crop of musicians in the world, but it was bringing those artists to the kind of attention it is impossible to imagine they would have received otherwise.

Dave Ball: Apart from Soft Cell and The The, most of Some Bizzare was quite revolutionary in a way. Stuff that would never get in the charts, but now at least people were listening to it and it was getting reviews.[8]

Stevo, speaking in 1988: Someone came up to me recently and said, 'Stevo, the trouble with you, your artistes and Some Bizzare is that you're too bigoted'. And I said, 'Yes, you're right, we are bigoted and we've got every right to be because we're superior'. The music of Some Bizzare is not a projection to the masses. It is something which is very self-indulgent. And yes, it's a shame that you're 'elite' if you put over music that's intelligent, original, and projects attitudes. Some Bizzare has got its own variety in a very anti-structured framework. Maybe you can compare Neubauten to Cabaret Voltaire or PTV to Foetus; to me, there is no comparison. We widen variety, we support creativity, we discourage sycophantic adulation.[9]

Annie Hogan: Stevo was a massive part of Soft Cell making it. I mean, I've got my opinions on him, but at the same time, he really created a whirlwind.[10]

Peter Ashworth, Soft Cell photographer: I think Stevo was very important in the creation of what Soft Cell became. He was so fucking barking that whatever Dave and Marc did was nothing compared to what Stevo was doing, and that allowed them to get away with quite a lot because they'd always blame the bloody manager.[11]

Daniel Miller: I've got a lot of respect for Stevo and for what he's done.

Newly ensconced at Phonogram thanks to Stevo, Soft Cell went into the studio with Daniel Miller to record their debut single proper, 'Memorabilia', a song written with the dance records that thumped from the Warehouse's pulsating speakers in mind.

Dave Ball: The *Mutant Moments* EP had been a little taster; it was never really supposed to be a serious record. Our first proper record was 'Memorabilia'.[12]

Marc Almond: It was based on a James Brown riff with a rap from me almost made up on the spot, a paean to obsession and collectable trash, a serial killer collecting little bits of you 'to show you I've been there'.[13]

Daniel Miller: We worked together well, the band and I. We had a similar sensibility, and a similar idea of where their songs could go, and I brought a bit of extra synth knowledge, even though I didn't have much. We had a lot in common, it wasn't a rock producer or a pop producer who had come in to try and work with them; we'd both come up from the underground. There was no budget, but it was a professional recording studio which felt like a luxury at that time. We were constantly watching the clock, so it had to be done fast, but I felt like the process benefitted from that. We didn't have too much time to dick around, and it went very smoothly.

Released in a somewhat unconventional manner, with 'Memorabilia' as the twelve-inch single and another song, 'A Man Could Get Lost' as the seven-inch, it was the former that was by far their biggest priority, as the format was angled towards the club scene.

Daniel Miller: The charts were so far away from what we were doing at that time, a totally different world, so we weren't going for a chart record. We wanted to make it a dancefloor record, something people could play in the so-called Futurist or New Romantic clubs. It did get a good response, as far as I can remember.

Rusty Egan: That was the gamechanger for me, that fucking record. I thought, 'This is the sound of the future! This is how a record should be!'

Ian Dewhirst: I didn't 'get' Soft Cell on *Mutant Moments*. I just thought, 'No, this doesn't fit with anything, it's too left field and too amateurish.' But when 'Memorabilia' came out, that was what made them a group to watch to me. It was just a huge record at the Warehouse, it took everything up a notch.

At the same time, Soft Cell had been forced to step up their live set. Their first performance in London, at Cabaret Futura, had been good, albeit unspectacular.

Richard Strange: I mainly remember that the Pogues played the same night. Although Marc was very charismatic, the synthesisers back then were fairly crude and monophonic – you'd play them with two fingers and put the other two fingers up to the music business.

A set at Crocs nightclub in Rayleigh, Essex, however, would prove disastrous. Soft Cell had been booked to follow the venue's house band, Depeche Mode.

Dave Ball: I remember watching them soundcheck. They were fantastic, younger than us and so much better. Then Marc and I, the main band, we just had a dreadful gig. The sound was shit, we were shit. We'd been in some magazines, Soft Cell and Depeche Mode were 'the faces', 'the ones to watch', so all these people from London – Visage, Spandau Ballet, all their Blitz Kid friends – they had all turned up to watch these two bands who were going to conquer the world of electronic music. They were booing us off and chucking coins at us!

Driving back to Leeds in a transit van afterwards, that was when we decided we were going to have to up our ante. We decided to get the backing tracks properly sorted out, our image properly sorted out. We managed to blag some money from the record company and completely rethought it.[14]

They also enlisted help from Huw Feather, along with his partner, Liz Pugh, to provide proper staging for their show: a white padded cell as an obvious play on the band's name, with pink and blue neon bars. It was the genesis point for a visual identity that would eventually become iconic, and a masterpiece in presenting a bold statement on a minimal budget. Here, Feather's own arts education held sway in Soft Cell's early visuals as crucially as Almond and Ball's did in their music.

Huw Feather: In Nottingham I was doing lots of odd, esoteric, avant-garde theatre, which is perfect for developing your chops as a theatre designer. There was an interest in being camp, but using it as a tool, rather than an end point.

Dave Ball: We also nicked a Revox from the A&R department at Phonogram and jumped into a taxi because my machine wouldn't take the larger spools that we needed. Afterwards we did a gig at a place called the Venue in Victoria, which was owned by Richard Branson, and things started to turn around for us. We got our act together professionally, and we were becoming quite hip with the London movers and shakers.[15]

Brian Moss: We'd hire a short-wheel transit van and pack all the stuff in there. Usually, Josephine would be in the front and Dave and Marc would be in the back. We had to put together the padded cell on stage; everything was in the van, no road crew or anything like that, no glamour apart from the actual gig. We played Rock City in Nottingham – that was a really busy night, packed out with seven or eight hundred people.

Part of a tour in the spring of 1981, the Rock City gig would see so many fans invading the stage that the padded cell would collapse, the neon bars smashing on the stage floor. At a homecoming show at Amnesia, meanwhile, the band turned away almost two hundred fans who had failed to get in. Faced with a similar situation not long afterwards, the enterprising owner of the Retford Porterhouse charged some fans full price simply for the privilege of watching Soft Cell play on the downstairs CCTV monitors.

Dave Ball: We were getting proper press people turning up and actually liking it, too, in particular Betty Page [aka Beverley Glick] and Tony Mitchell from *Sounds*.[16]

Beverley Glick: It was the heat of that New Romantic thing, but I never felt part of that scene. It was all quite cliquey. But when I met Marc and Dave, they never felt part of it either, especially because they weren't from London and it was a very London-centric scene. I connected with them because I felt like I was an outsider too. I didn't have a background in journalism – I'd been a secretary, and women were still in the minority. Soft Cell were funny, they were real, they weren't judging me like I felt some of the London people were.

Marc Almond: We had formed from post-punk and the northern electronic scene of Sheffield and Leeds. London was more fashion conscious and superficial; Soft Cell were a transgressive electronic punk band, more in common with Suicide, or Throbbing Gristle with catchy tunes. We were more about social comment, and sometimes sardonic and satirical.[17]

Not only were Soft Cell finally becoming a finely tuned live act, 'Memorabilia' was finding the success Soft Cell had intended in the club scene. Across the Atlantic it became a crossover hit, played as much in clubs with a predominantly Black clientele as White, reaching number thirty-five in the Billboard dance club charts and laying the groundwork for the deeper relationship between Soft Cell and New York that was to follow. It was also enough to give the ever-sceptical Phonogram cause to keep them on the books.

Marc Almond: We were very pleased when it was played around the clubs and Rusty Egan was mixing thirty-minute mixes of it. It's since been called the first acid house record, and I was most thrilled when Black guys in New York clubs and even on the street came up to me and said how much they loved the record.[18]

Dave Ball: I think Phonogram must have seen that and thought, 'Hang on, these two oiks from Leeds are getting played in New York? Let's give them another chance.'[19]

Though it was not the chart success that Phonogram had been hoping for, the reputation 'Memorabilia' garnered in the clubs was enough for them to offer one more swing at a bona fide hit. A hit their next single would be, a hit so gargantuan, so monstrously huge, that it would swallow the band whole.

'Tainted Love' was not merely an unexpected number-one single for an art school band. It is the kind of song so pervasive that it is now used as cultural shorthand for an entire generation of pop music. Soft Cell's next four singles were each to break the top five, yet from forty years' distance their first and only number one continues, for the casual listener at least, to dwarf the band that recorded it.

Dave Ball: Even grandparents have heard 'Tainted Love'. They've heard of 'Tainted Love', but they've not heard of your band. People come up to me and say, 'What band are you in?' I say, 'Soft Cell', and they go, 'I've never heard of Soft Cell.' I say, 'You heard of "Tainted Love?"' And they say, 'Oh yeah! "Tainted Love!"'[1]

As with any such song, relentless repetition has dulled its charms, yet in retrospect it seems obvious that 'Tainted Love' should be a smash. Lyrics that appear straightforward and accessible conceal a narrative that runs the emotional gamut, pushing and pulling between desire and repulsion. Its 'da dun dun' hook is irresistible. Yet Soft Cell's version was in fact the song's fourth attempt at mass appeal. When it was originally written by Ed Cobb for then-teenager Gloria Jones as the B-side to her 1965 single 'My Bad Boy's Comin' Home', it failed to chart on either side of the Atlantic. For the time being, it was a swiftly forgotten flop.

To become the all-conquering pop goliath that Soft Cell would release in 1981, this old forgotten song would require two separate charges to reach a teenage Dave Ball at around the same time. One was the electronic magic of a Kraftwerk cassette, played to him by his colleague in the ice cream factory one lazy, rainy day in the mid-1970s. The other was the raw energy of the Northern Soul movement, which was simultaneously reaching its crescendo right on his doorstep at the Blackpool Mecca. There, forgotten songs were revived by rabid rarity-hunters, scouring America for their next hit of obscure up-tempo soul, returning to the north of England to unleash what they had found. Jones's 'Tainted Love' was one such treasure, reclaimed at last as a hit – albeit only in this specific scene.

In many ways these two musical movements were total opposites – Kraftwerk looked forwards to futuristic new sounds while Northern Soul looked backwards to the 1960s; Kraftwerk portrayed themselves with robotic restraint, while the Northern Soulers hosted all-night parties that were primal – almost feral – in their energy. The former was the immovable object, the latter the unstoppable force, and when at last they collided in Ball's head, it was from the sparks that he crafted the song that was to follow him for the rest of his life.

Bedsit Land

'Tainted Love' might never have reached Ball at all had Blackpool not emerged, along with the Wigan Casino barely twenty-five miles away, as one of Northern Soul's two duelling zeniths by the time he reached his teens. It was the culmination of a decade's worth of growth which can broadly be traced back to British mod culture's embrace in the mid-1960s of Black American soul music. At that point it was led by the Motown sound, where lyrics of deep longing juxtaposed beautifully with punchy, direct and danceable up-tempo beats. Its fandom in Britain was London-centric at first, but before long underground clubs like Sheffield's Mojo and Manchester's Twisted Wheel had emerged as the scene's northern outposts.[2] The Black American zeitgeist grew more political at the end of the decade, however, evolving alongside protests at the 1968 Olympics, the Watts riots and the murder of Martin Luther King Jr., with Black GIs returning from the Vietnam War newly militarised by their experience. As a result, the old Motown sound began to fade in favour of something funkier, more complex and more political.

A divergence began to appear in the young Britons who were listening from a distance. In the south, clubbers embraced that new sound, as well as the parallel burgeoning of psychedelic music, but in the northern clubs it failed to take hold. For them, the music they sought was simply getting faster and faster.

Ian Dewhirst: Roger Eagle at the Twisted Wheel began to notice a phenomenon where the higher-tempo stuff was hitting big with the next generation of kids coming onto the scene. As to why this happened in the north of England more so than the south, it might be a bit of a cliché but in the north they worked hard and they played hard. If someone's working at a steel foundry in Sheffield from six in the morning until five in the afternoon, they're not going to want to go to a Tiffanys 'til one or two in the morning with the local dorks. They want to get some speed down their neck and dance all night to million-miles-an-hour stuff.

I'd go down to London to find records, and I was dipping in and out of places there too, but it was a completely different vibe. The crowd were fashionable. You'd be hearing soul music, but it was the funkier variety. You'd never hear James Brown if you were up north. I think southerners looked at the northern scene as being slightly unsophisticated because the music was more dated.

At the Twisted Wheel, the intensity of the music was matched by the intensity of the crowd, many of whom were taking stolen prescription amphetamines. After the venue was closed amid related pressure from the city council, in Blackpool a precocious teenage soul collector called Ian Levine convinced DJ Tony Jebb to turn his commercial soul nights at the Highland Room at the top of the Mecca entertainment complex into Northern Soul events.

Ian Levine, Blackpool Mecca DJ: I said to him, 'There's hundreds and hundreds of people who've got nowhere to go. I'll lend you my records if you turn the Highland Room into a Northern Soul night.' I had an amazing record collection by then.[3]

The Mecca's relatively sedate closing time of 2 a.m., however, meant that it was Chris Burton's venue, the Golden Torch in Tunstall, Stoke-on-Trent, that emerged as the Twisted Wheel's first successor. Regularly swapping DJs with the Mecca, it hosted crowds more than twice its five-hundred-person capacity for monthly, then weekly allnighters, which lasted from 8 p.m. on Saturdays until 8 a.m. on Sundays, as well as live shows from many of the scene's American stars.

Ian Levine: The Torch became so popular that eventually Tony Jebb moved down there to become the head DJ. At that time, he was the scene's first superstar DJ. He was totally against the norm with hair down to his shoulders, dark-blue sunglasses and crushed velvet trousers. But by December 1972, Tony had been busted for selling drugs and Chris Burton was facing trouble from the council, who wanted to shut the place down. Not only were people breaking into chemists on the way down, they were stealing milk from people's porches on the way back.

By the time Dave Ball entered his teens, his hometown had finally emerged as the pinnacle of the Northern Soul scene, with Levine and another DJ, Colin Curtis, firmly ensconced as the head DJs.

Ian Dewhirst: When the Torch closed, all of a sudden it was 'OK, where's gonna take up the slack?', and so Blackpool filled that void until the Wigan Casino opened slightly later. And even then, the Mecca was where you went to really be ahead.

Da dun dun

Colin Curtis, Blackpool Mecca DJ: The Blackpool Mecca was a huge building. As you went in, there were bridal shops and ten-pin bowling, all part of the complex, but on the right-hand side there was a door. Through there you'd go up two escalators and then again up another set of stairs. Through some glass doors there was then a hundred yards of tartan carpet, leading all the way down to the Highland Room. That was where people would chat or fall over because they had taken too many drugs or whatever, a magical place. Then the room itself had a low roof, a capacity of six to eight hundred, with speakers around the room all pointing towards the dancefloor.[4]

Ian Dewhirst: Levine and Curtis were like hounds; there was no stone left unturned. You'd have to go every weekend because the turnover of records at that point was so quick. Levine was that far ahead he was untouchable. Because he was from a rich family, he was in the States three or four times a year, doing nothing but running around record shops and picking up the most incredible stuff.

Because of the Mecca's earlier closing time compared to its predecessors, amphetamine usage was rather less dramatic there than it had been at the Twisted Wheel and the Torch's all-nighters. Nevertheless, nights there still fizzed with energy.

Dave Ball: What appealed to me was the spirit of the time. It was exotic because it was American, and I had always liked Motown that I'd heard on Radio 1. It was an extension of that, all these little American companies trying to emulate

Motown's success. I just thought the whole thing was great. I liked the clothes, and the dancing was really energetic. It was a weird culture clash that I found very exciting.[5]

Colin Curtis: It's the classic 'White guys can't dance', so they developed this strange technique, spinning around, running across the floor and back again.

Ian Dewhirst: A lot of these guys were hard guys. I was a grammar school boy but I was knocking around with factory workers. They'd be coming home at five o'clock, covered in filth, getting themselves scrubbed up, getting the suit on, and looking the business. They used to pride themselves on how they looked. And then the dancing was incredibly, incredibly athletic. You had to be at the peak of fitness to do it properly. There was one guy at the Wheel called Frank Booper who pioneered running up a wall then going down into a backdrop. There was another guy from Bradford called Andy Simpson, he was a spectacular dancer and he had long hair, almost like a hippie, and he specialised in aeroplane spins. His hair would whip people in the face as he was spinning around, the sweat would fly off him and cover everyone in the room.

Ian Levine: A load of wankers who don't know what the fuck they're talking about have later said they were trying to do kung fu moves like Bruce Lee. But the dancing comes directly from the soul groups that visited the Twisted Wheel. Jackie Wilson in particular, his backdrops and spins. Even a bit of James Brown, although he wasn't Northern Soul. The early dancers would practise all week in front of their mirrors.

Da dun dun

There was a flamboyance to Northern Soul – particularly for men, where high kicks and backflips were not just permitted but encouraged – that was at odds with other options for nightlife in the working-class communities that the nights were springing up; clubs like the Mecca and Wigan Casino were as much an exercise in forging a new reality as those in Leeds, London and New York that Ball was to experience later on.

Ian Dewhirst: It was a way of showing off. Peacocks, strutting their stuff.

Colin Curtis: A local club in Stoke-on-Trent booked me to DJ once, but it fell apart because they said that the guys wouldn't be allowed to dance on their own, they'd have to dance with a woman.

Ian Levine: I went to a wedding once and was dancing the Northern Soul moves – they were horrified!

Integral as fashion, drugs and dancing were to Northern Soul, these elements were secondary to the music being played. More than perhaps any other scene in music history to that point, obscurity was king. Because the kind of records the northerners valued were no longer being made, DJs went to greater and greater lengths to find ever-more-obscure examples of the sound. Long-forgotten flops recorded by Motown-imitating upstarts across America, whose work could never find a wide audience in the pre-internet days of limited distribution, suddenly became hits, taking on a new life thanks to the obsessive fandom of an audience they might never have imagined. Such was Ian Levine's obsession that on one family holiday to America, he picked up so many records that an onward flight to the Caribbean struggled to take off.

Ian Levine: I bought four thousand records from Goodwill shops that a local radio station had donated their stock to. They were all radio station promos that record companies had sent throughout the 1960s. In that collection was every Northern Soul record that ever went big, ever. I was determined to go through every single one, I didn't want to miss even one decent record, many of which are still among the biggest to this day. All the staple classics came from that load.

Colin Curtis: All these artists had been forgotten about. In this country you put out a record and everywhere from Land's End to John O'Groats knows it's out. But over in America there were regional hits, people trying to earn a living off the back of the Motown sound.

Ian Levine: Only about one out of five hundred people [at the Highland Room] was Black. It was a White, working-class audience, and all these White kids were dancing to Black American music, made by people who wanted to be Diana Ross, Marvin Gaye or the Supremes, who had put a record out on their own tiny little label but never got national distribution so never got themselves heard. Tony Cummings [of *Black Music* magazine] used to write about how he fantasised about Eddie Foster in San Francisco, dreaming that somewhere in the world, five thousand White kids were dancing to his records. Then he'd wake up and think, 'What a stupid idea!' But it was happening!

One such song that became a hit on the Northern Soul scene was 'Tainted Love' – that old flop by Ed Cobb, now suddenly revitalised.

Gloria Jones: If I had known that 'Tainted Love' had been accepted in England when I was a teenager, I would have gone there! It would have given me a career! But no one ever told me that it was a hit over there. I never liked the song. I was a minister's daughter, coming out of the Church of God in Christ who were your holy rollers who didn't believe in makeup, going to the show or kissing, and the word 'tainted' was very offensive. When they said they were going to put that song on the B-side, I was like, 'Oh, no!' But they wanted to go with 'Tainted Love'. Sorry about that, Dad![6]

Ian Dewhirst: 'Tainted Love' was one of those records that broke almost simultaneously around the country. All the key DJs had it, and it was super-fast, a great floor-filler. Before long it transcended out of the Northern Soul scene. I heard that the first pressing of the bootleg sold twenty thousand copies. The song permeated out to the B- and C-list DJs. The guys that were running the Northern Soul night in their local town on a Tuesday night would be all be playing Gloria Jones.

Jones attempted to capitalise on the resurgence of 'Tainted Love' via a 1976 re-record, but once again it failed to chart, likewise a 1975 cover by Bolton teenager Ruth Swann.

Trying to exploit the Northern Soul phenomenon, in 1975 a band called Sparkle renamed themselves 'Wigan's Ovation' and recorded a version of the Invitations' 'Skiing in the Snow'. This became a hit, marking the moment the Northern Soul otherworld went mainstream. Two years later, Granada Television broadcast a documentary about Wigan Casino that was watched by twenty million people, leading to such a surge in interest that the venue had to close applications for membership altogether.

All the while, the immense well of obscure 1960s hits was at long last drying up. The Casino DJs lowered their standards in search of anything with a beat remotely resembling the classic Northern Soul rhythm; even the likes of Radio 1 DJ Tony Blackburn's long-forgotten 1968 cover of 'I'll Do Anything' became fair game. Ian Levine in Blackpool, meanwhile, incorporated the sounds of New York's blossoming disco scene into the Mecca's soundtrack – relying on the links between the new music's upbeat rhythm and those of vintage Motown – a decision so controversial that his sets became sites of protests.

Ian Levine: We would do a set on Sundays at the Ritz in Manchester and so did Richard Searling from Wigan Casino. When I was on the crowd would be chanting, 'Get off! We want Searling!' and when he was on it was, 'Get off! We want Levine!'

By the time Soft Cell were making their early music, the Northern Soul scene had faded. Levine had departed altogether to become one of the first DJs at the new London gay club Heaven. Ball, too, had moved on, in his case towards the burgeoning punk, performance art and electronica scenes from which the band was formed. The sound of classic Northern Soul had not quite left him, however.

Ian Levine: Northern Soul. Once it's in your blood you can never get rid of it. You can go off and do something else, have kids, a career, but you will always return to it. You'll always go back in the end.

Marc Almond, meanwhile, had been introduced to the genre inadvertently one night at the Warehouse in Leeds, where Ian Dewhirst was now DJing.

Ian Dewhirst: By then I had long left the Northern Soul scene and moved onto disco and jazz funk, but one day at the Warehouse we had Q-Tips on, Paul Young's R&B covers band before he went solo. It was his birthday that night, and Mike Wiand suggested we do something special. Usually, the acts came on at about ten thirty to eleven, so there were a couple of hours beforehand where people were just drinking and waiting for the band. I decided to pull out all the Northern Soul stuff, stuff that I hadn't played for about four or five years. It was about half nine, and the place was filling up nicely when I put 'Tainted Love' on. It sounded so fantastic over the Warehouse speaker system. The DJ booth was up some stairs and enclosed, almost like a pulpit with a lockable door, and about thirty seconds of the way into the song I spotted Marc Almond haring up to the DJ booth from the cloakroom. I'm thinking, 'What's going on? Is he gonna have a row with someone?' He was saying 'What's this record?

What's this record? You've got to tape it for me!' I thought, 'Wow. That's some effect!'

Marc Almond: It's dancing your tears away, dancing your pain away, you're on the dance floor dancing to a dance beat but you're hearing this singer singing about a lost love, the pain of life, a heartbreak. 'I'm gonna have a good time and leave all my heartbreak, all my pain behind.' That bittersweet feeling of good times to escape from the bad times [...] We were looking for a cover version to put in the set, and at the time, for electronic bands it was the thing to be very cool. Everything was bleak; this cold, northern, robotic thing. And Dave Ball suggested to me, what about 'Tainted Love'? [...] I thought that was what Soft Cell was all about: Tainted and Love. These two words together. Something about the song just hooked me in.[7]

Dave Ball: 'Tainted Love' was a track we used in our live set and it was very popular. 'Bedsitter' was also very popular in the early days too, before it came out as a single.[8]

Marc Almond: It was Phonogram's decision to release 'Tainted Love'; a record company will go for the cover version as it's the easiest option. Even Phonogram didn't have a lot of faith in it really or us generally. They put us with producer Mike Thorne to record 'Tainted Love' and we did it in a day.[9]

Dave Ball: We had recorded a demo of 'Tainted Love' with Daniel Miller, but Phonogram thought it sounded too mechanical. Because they had seen how 'Memorabilia' had gone down really well in the clubs and was getting noticed in New

York, they said 'we'll give you a second chance, but the condition is we want to bring in our own producer, Mike Thorne'.[10]

Daniel Miller: I don't actually remember [recording a demo of 'Tainted Love'] at all. I'm not denying it, I just don't remember it. Maybe I just blanked it out because I didn't end up doing the final version! I thought we'd all done a good job together, but [Thorne] was a much more experienced producer than me.

Mike Thorne happened to be in London at the time, along with all his gear, including one of the first Sinclavier digital synthesisers, to record the soundtrack to the film *Memoirs of a Survivor*. Phonogram asked if he would be interested in recording a couple of singles on the side, B-Movie's 'Remembrance Day' and Soft Cell's 'Tainted Love'.

Mike Thorne: I thought Gloria Jones's version of it wasn't up to much at all. The [Daniel Miller] demo from Soft Cell seemed to sing the song a lot better. It was more with the spirit of the song – there was regret in it. The Jones version might as well have been recorded on speed it was so over the top and hyperactive.[11]

Daniel Miller: I think Mike Thorne did a brilliant job. 'Tainted Love' was a brilliant production, and that was a really great creative relationship.

Ian Dewhirst: I think I first heard about it from Annie. 'Do you know, Marc's going to do a cover of "Tainted Love"?' I've got to be honest, I couldn't see it. I was thinking, 'Christ, of all the songs he could have covered.' Of course, I wasn't thinking that they'd slow it down, use a completely different set of production values.

For the twelve-inch version, Soft Cell turned it into a medley that blended with the Supremes' 'Where Did Our Love Go', a decision that would not only add to the purists' ire, but come to haunt them financially.

John Keenan: I remember having a conversation with Dave one night, saying 'If you'd put one of your own songs you would have got just as much royalties!' Dave said it was just a rookie error, they didn't twig that they could've made even more money.

Brian Moss: I think Mike Wiand said they would have instantly been millionaires if they'd put one of their own songs on the B-side. But we were all young kids; we were all so green.

Beverley Glick: Nobody was expecting 'Tainted Love' to be a hit. I think Phonogram were about to drop them. It took everybody by surprise how huge it was.

Ian Levine: I thought that Soft Cell's 'Tainted Love' was a travesty. It took all the soul out of it. Their music left me cold.

Colin Bell, Head of Publicity, Phonogram: The purists thought it was comedy. You couldn't paint Marc Almond in the same light as Gloria Jones![12]

Da dun dun

Almond was certainly no powerhouse vocalist in the lineage of Jones or the Supremes; as Soft Cell later grew in prominence, his bum notes and wobbles out of key would make him the subject of ridicule. But as Thorne recognised during the recording of 'Tainted Love', his singing still possessed a soulfulness to rival any of the greats.

Mike Thorne: At that point there were so many productions being made that were perfectly in tune. Everything was spot on, so the producers thought 'it must be OK'. But I trusted myself a bit more than that. I relied on the hairs on my forearm. If a performance came in that made the hairs raise, then that was the one. I had been around the houses, worked in pop and classical music, so I was confident enough to trust my instant judgement, and that was what happened with the long version of 'Tainted Love'. We were doing a soundcheck. Off we went and the engineer said, 'That's it, I've got all I need', but I said, 'No! Keep it going! He's singing his heart out!' So we kept going for the whole nine minutes all the way to the end. Marc was grumbling later about how I'd let out-of-tune-ness slip through, but I was responding to the emotion that was coming out of the speakers.[13]

It would be that soulfulness that would help set Soft Cell apart from the pack; a human touch to juxtapose the coldness of the synthesiser sound that was coming to dominate pop.

Beverley Glick: I connected with Soft Cell because they were real; they seemed authentic.

Josephine Warden: When you know that there's truth in something, you can relate to it, and I know that every single line he wrote he was passionate about, or he'd thought about, or he was laughing about. Because it was honest, it was easy to latch on to; there was a clarity about what he did. It was all from the heart and truthful and honest.[14]

The way 'Tainted Love' sounds instrumentally, meanwhile, is symbolic of the stage Soft Cell were at when they recorded it – scrappy upstarts, transforming before one's ears into uncomfortable megastars. Its hypnotic, looping bassline is sourced from Ball's cheap Korg synthesiser, but the earworm 'da dun dun' synth stabs come from Thorne's £120,000 Synclavier.

Mike Thorne: I took my cue from what they were doing and accommodated. You read about producers who have a sound but that's something I've always avoided. I want to have the sound of the band, and a sound that amplifies the band. I don't want to impose at all. We sat around the control room after we'd finished mixing it, and thought, 'This could be a cult hit!'[15]

Annie Hogan: I remember Soft Cell playing at Amnesia, and Marc saying, 'This is our next single', and them doing 'Tainted Love'. It sounded amazing.[16]

Brian Moss: We were backstage with Marc and Dave, and Marc said, 'Do you want to do backing vocals?'. He wrote them down on a napkin and said 'follow me, repeat these lines'.

Da dun dun

Josephine Warden: I said, 'Fuck off, I'm not learning your songs!' But he said, 'Just follow me. When I say "Memorabilia", you say "Memorabilia". For "Tainted Love", you'll know what to do.'[17]

Ian Dewhirst: Marc actually brought me the acetate of 'Tainted Love'; literally got off the train from London, brought it into Amnesia and said, 'Alright, do you wanna hear this? It's our version of "Tainted Love".' As soon as I heard it, well let's just say I knew it was a hit. It flew off the turntable and sounded absolutely incredible. I was absolutely knocked out. I couldn't believe that he'd turned this song from an archetypal 1960s stomper into a record that sounded exactly right for now. For that early electro glam crowd it sounded commercial as hell. Doing 'Where Did Our Love Go?' with it wouldn't have been any good royalty wise, but as a record it works like an absolute dream.

Brian Moss: It would pack the dancefloor every time we played it. It was massive, and it was still going to shoot to this height that we couldn't grasp.

Annie Hogan: I could play 'Tainted Love' four times a night, easily, and I was only on from seven 'til ten!'[18]

'Tainted Love' entered the charts at number sixty-two on 1 August 1981, two weeks after its release. A week later it was at forty-five, and the week after that it reached number twenty-six. By cracking the top forty, Soft Cell earnt themselves the opportunity of their lives: an appearance on *Top of the Pops*.

Bedsit Land

Marc Almond: When it started to move into and up the charts it was a bit of a shock. Thrilling too, but life felt like it was never going to be the same.[19]

Chapter 6
TOP OF THE POPS

Annie Hogan was at home in the complex of bedsits on Leicester Grove in Leeds when she received a phone call from Marc Almond to let her know he had arrived safely at the BBC's Television Centre.

Annie Hogan: At that point he was still living in Leeds, still coming on our nights out. *Top of the Pops* was this unbelievably exciting thing. It was massive, very influential back then. I mean, now it just looks archaic, but back then it was the thing. You had *The Old Grey Whistle Test*, but *Top of the Pops* was the biggie.[1]

Ian Gittins, journalist, *Top of the Pops* chronicler: *Top of the Pops* was absolutely enormous. The biggest thing you could imagine, the one chance a band had to play their music on TV to a huge audience. Bands would be on tour in America, but if they were offered *Top of the Pops* they would fly back just for one day to do it because the sales would be so astronomic. In 1981 it was pretty much the peak of the show. *The Tube* didn't come along until later, *The Old Grey Whistle Test* was what your dad watched, and MTV [when it launched later in 1981] was on cable, which most people didn't have. It's impossible to overstate just how crucial *Top of the Pops* was to bands, and to the music industry. Part of it was also your dad going, 'What's he bloody dressed like?! Is it a boy or a girl?'[2]

More aware than anyone of the opportunity on offer were Phonogram. There had been a frostiness between them and Soft Cell from the start – Stevo had only secured the band a deal by throwing them into the pot with B-Movie, after all – but now the tension between the two was becoming fully apparent.

Roy Gould, floor manager, *Top of the Pops*: First thing on Tuesday morning, two days before filming, I'd be sat on the end of a phone, listening to the charts coming in, and all the labels' pluggers would be there too, leaning over my shoulder to hear whether their band had gone up or down. If they'd gone up, they'd be straight onto hassling the producer, which was then Michael Hurll, seeing if they could get their band on the show.[3]

Dave Ball: When we got to Phonogram's office on New Bond Street, they said, 'We're going to have to do camera rehearsals. When that red light comes on, that's the camera. You have to look into the camera!' Blah blah blah. I was trained to make sure I hit the drums at the right time. It was all very forced and all very staged. There was a lot of resistance to us from the record company. They said that Marc shouldn't wear makeup and bangles.[4]

Marc Almond: We were odd, and they didn't really get us.[5]

Dave Ball: They wanted us to have a drummer and a bass guitarist. I don't think they really got the concept. The public got it straight away, but the record companies – even after this era of supposedly radical punk bands – they didn't get it at all.[6]

Roy Gould: We'd get a list from the record pluggers of what instruments we'd need for the show, and we'd rent them from a music shop in West London called Maurice Plaquet. I can't remember if it was Soft Cell or one of the other early synth pop bands, but when we asked for a synth stand they didn't even have one. We had to put it on a flight case.

Soft Cell's first *Top of the Pops* appearance is anxious and spikey. Almond moves with uncomfortable, pent-up energy, his Northern Soul handclaps rehearsed painstakingly to hit the beat. Although he is only miming, Ball chews gum and looks down coyly at his keyboard for the entire performance, save for a few nervous glances towards his bandmate. Despite Phonogram's rehearsals the electronic drum pad in front of him goes almost entirely unhit.

Roy Gould: All the bands were like rats in the middle of a road – they were so frightened because this was a huge deal. This was make or break. When I was floor assistant, part of that was running, and I had to get the bands out of their dressing rooms. It was probably their first time in a television studio. The old hands like Status Quo and all those were quite blasé, but the groups like Soft Cell, they were very, very nervous. At that time the pop industry was very much in flux.

I'm a child of the 1960s; I grew up with guitar bands, but the synth-based groups were very different from the bands like Status Quo and Slade, who had perfected a stage presence and were playing to the crowd. Bands like Soft Cell and the Human League were a different animal, a softer, different, more internal style.

Awkward though it was, their performance had enough of an effect that within a week the song rose to number nine, after that to number two, and by 5 September 1981 it sat at long last at number one. Reflecting their rapid success, the band were invited to perform 'Tainted Love' on *Top of the Pops* for a second time.

Marc Almond: I remember the record company instructing me which camera to look to for my second appearance, and they told me to ditch the look.[7]

Colin Bell: I was kind of a freak in the record business at that time because I was one of the few openly gay executives. Because of that I was instructed, 'Can you go down to *Top of the Pops* as the only person who's gay, and see if you can control how camp they appear?' What they meant was, can you try and control the leather? I got to the dressing room and thought, there's no point. They're going to wear what they're going to wear. I don't know if I even said anything to them. And of course, it was sensational. It was exactly the right thing for them to wear.

Marc Almond: I ignored them, and I was right to do so.[8]

Barely a month had passed between Soft Cell's first and second *Top of the Pops* tapings, but the band's transformation was already clear to see. Almond begins with his back to crowd, and as he spins, he reveals that his bangles and chains have tripled in quantity, his eyeliner has thickened tenfold. His moves no longer feel awkwardly timed to fit the song, but an extension of its narrative, dramatic flourishes and a teasing look directly down the barrel of the camera.

Marc Almond: Like Bolan and Bowie had illuminated my life, I since found out that I had such an effect on others. They felt they weren't alone.[9]

Angela Smith, *Top of the Pops* viewer: I was seventeen. I liked quite a range of different things, but I'd never been really passionate about anything before. The first time I heard 'Tainted Love' on *Top of the Pops* I responded in a different way. I wanted to hear more, immediately. I can remember it quite clearly, despite the years. It was an all-encompassing performance. The visual contrast between Marc Almond and Dave Ball was very striking. Dave looked more conventional, much more of a background figure but still very much part of the experience. Marc was captivating. I hadn't seen anything like him before. All the black, clothes, hair, eye makeup, his jewellery and the way he made eye contact with the camera. His startlingly androgynous appearance was compelling. But mostly it was his voice that drew me in and I've been there ever since. Later on, Marc did things that expanded his vocal range in more challenging ways than 'Tainted Love', but as a reworking, the old Gloria Jones classic was completely electrified and electrifying, it was a perfect vehicle for his voice at the moment. Everything was balanced.[10]

Tim Arnold, *Top of the Pops* viewer: I was only six, but I remember seeing him on *Top of the Pops*. It was the first time I saw someone on television where his gender didn't seem to register. I only realised this years later, but what I saw was spirit, talent. He had such an original physicality on stage, and the voice was so unaffected. There was no reference point.[11]

It was the darkness that Soft Cell wove beneath the pop veneer of 'Tainted Love' that made it especially transfixing – a dash of the sinister to Almond's gaze down the camera and all-black outfit. It was also, if not completely explicit, obvious in its gayness.

Dave Ball: I think a lot of people, gay or otherwise, related to it. It was quite obvious to everyone that Marc was gay. Even though we weren't allowed to talk about it, it certainly empowered a lot of gay young men. A lot of people said this to us – they felt like they weren't alone. If you live in some little town and you're having feelings towards your own sex, you probably feel a bit alienated by your mates at school going on about girls. I can't speak from experience, but it must feel quite alienating. I think he empowered those people, made them feel like they're not the only one.

It was quite obvious that Marc was camp to say the least, but people were like 'Well, he's just like David Bowie or Alice Cooper, isn't he? He just wears makeup!' But because Marc wore all black as well, he was a bit more scary.[12]

Cathi Unsworth, *Top of the Pops* viewer, chronicler of goth: For me, Marc and Soft Cell were my goth gateway. I saw them doing 'Tainted Love' on *Top of the Pops* and that was it – wherever they were going, I wanted to follow. Unlike the rest of the synth groups around at the time, there was something much more dangerous and compelling about Marc's voice and general sartorial appearance, Dave's spiv demeanour and the whole sound they conjured up.

Marc was sending out signals to all confused teenagers about their sexuality, that they were not alone, and that actually it was better to be a freak than a square. That is really important. There was no such thing as any gay club or pub where I came from – a similar place to Marc and Dave, the seaside, in my case Great Yarmouth – and it was really dangerous to flaunt any difference in front of the knuckle-draggers.[13]

Beverley Glick: People often talk about the moment they saw David Bowie doing 'Starman', and I think Marc probably had the same effect on a lot of young people at that time. But then I don't think Bowie ever got quite that level of backlash. Marc got an enormous amount of people being homophobic towards him. He would get comments like 'dirty little pervert' in a way that Boy George would never have done at that time. George managed to project this cuddly ragdoll image, he wasn't parading his sexuality, but people thought Marc was. And David Bowie was married, so he had that going for him!

'Tainted Love' would go on to sell over a million copies in 1981 alone, the most out of any song that year. By the following year it found success in America too, and stayed on the Billboard Hot 100 for a record breaking forty-three weeks. The band Phonogram had signed as an afterthought, that had hitherto been content to pursue an experimental art school sound and were still living in a Leeds bedsit, had become bona fide megastars.

Brian Moss: Once it was number one, we went round to Marc and Dave's flat, and there were all these followers outside. They'd spray-painted 'SOFT CELL LIVES HERE' on the wall. We had to navigate through all these people trying to get a glimpse of Marc and Dave – they still had their giro cheques pinned to the wall that they hadn't cashed! Obviously, they had to get out of there.

Ian Gittins: I moved to Leeds just as Soft Cell were getting massive. There was a weird relationship between the city and Marc Almond. For the kind of student I was – at Le Phonographique and the Warehouse every night, reading *NME* every week – he was a local boy done good, a hero figure. But at the same time there was something about his persona, exotic and quite tacky at the same time, that didn't fit in early 1980s West Yorkshire. Walking around Leeds he'd get two very mixed reactions: 'Oh my God, can I have your autograph?' and 'You fucking poof'. I got smacked in the face a couple of times just for having a peroxide quiff. He must have had it a million times worse.

Dave Ball: As soon as we got famous, the front door was locked; there was graffiti and a lot of envy and jealousy. We just had to move. I got a new flat where no one knew where it was.[14]

Annie Hogan: Marc bought a house and asked me to move in. I just remember thinking, 'Yes! Sounds fucking amazing!'[15]

Marc Almond: The *Top of the Pops* appearances totally transformed my life, both of our lives, but with it came a horrible side of fame. I've never liked crowds of people and I'm not able to be socially comfortable in many situations. I like to be quite private in many ways and I felt exposed, my life stolen from me and turned into something I didn't recognise. It wasn't mine anymore. It happened overnight. I've always said that I caused extreme reactions in people, they either wanted to marry me, mother me, murder me or fuck me. I attracted obsessives and stalkers, had untrue stories told about me to the press, became a freak magnet. Also came some terrible homophobia even from within my record company, even from those I knew to be gay. I was certainly damaged by it at the time and I handled fame initially very badly. I think we both did. Art students in a commercial corporate world.[16]

Dave Ball: To be quite blunt about it, there was a lot of homophobia around. Marc was told by the press office, 'When you're doing interviews, don't talk about sexuality'. There would be things in magazines like *Jackie*: 'Soft Cell, which one do you fancy? Big tall hunky Dave or little Marc?', and girls would write in saying which one they fancied the most.[17]

Annie Hogan: Marc was talking in interviews about his 'girlfriend Anne', you know? There was lots of pressure from Phonogram just because of the way he looked, and just how effeminate they thought he was. I think it was just very difficult.[18]

Phonogram attempted to toe a difficult line. Access to queer markets was valuable to them – a hit in gay clubs might have crossover potential when it came to 'mainstream' markets, and Almond's signalling to those scenes was beneficial. At the same time, they feared that an artist publicly proclaiming their homosexuality would be commercial suicide, especially given their plans to market Soft Cell as a mainstream pop band.

Richard Strange: It was still an anachronism – it was still the exception rather than the rule that you could be a gay or bisexual pop star. Because from Elvis Presley onwards, the audience for pop music was supposed to be young girls.

Annie Hogan: Obviously, they think that if he's out as gay they're not going to sell records. It's only ever about money. The anti-gay feeling and homophobia at the time was strong, while at the same time you've got a massive explosion of music and art with a huge gay influence. Even later, when I was in the band Cactus Rain in 1990, when the person who was singing in the band was my girlfriend, our record company sat down for a meeting with the manager – without me or her there – and said, 'What are we going to about these two being in a relationship?'[19]

Beverley Glick: Obviously everyone who knew Marc knew he was gay, but he was never explicit about his sexuality. He could never say he was gay because it would end his career. But it was kind of understood.

Colin Bell: If you wanted to have a career in music, your sexuality being known was seen as something that could stop it. People were nervous.

David Bowie might have been Almond's *Top of the Pops* reference point, but though Bowie had declared himself bisexual in a *Melody Maker* interview the same year as his 'Starman' performance, by 1983 he was keen to backtrack.

David Bowie, speaking to *Rolling Stone* in 1983: The biggest mistake I ever made […] was telling that *Melody Maker* writer that I was bisexual. Christ, I was so young then. I was experimenting.[20]

Colin Bell: Being openly gay, I was unusual in the record industry, but in the 1980s it turned out to be an asset. These heterosexual record companies could see where it was moving. They needed access to the gay market and to the gay clubs and to gay artists. Therefore, increasingly record companies looked to hire one or two gay people. I was probably the first. I had this theory – if you make records happen in the gay clubs, you can cross them over out of it.

Dave Ball: We were pin-up boys, believe it or not, even though it seems ridiculous now, Marc pretending to be a cute straight boy. You couldn't print the lyrics of 'Sex Dwarf' in *Jackie*; it wasn't little girls' music![21]

Colin Bell: Phonogram were not especially homophobic in the context of 1981. I think we were probably the most progressive with regard to sexuality, compared to all the others.

They were more understanding and cooler about it than just about anybody else in the industry. Nevertheless, received opinion was, 'If you're trying to sell records to little girls, you have to keep their sexuality a secret.' And that was what everybody did. Even Boy George and George Michael were heavily marketed as heterosexual, laughable as it might seem now. But for my generation, the process of coming to terms with your sexuality, actually going ahead and selling yourself as a gay guy was a terrifying prospect around that time. To say people were homophobic is technically true, but it also does them a great disservice. To stop being homophobic you have to start somewhere, you have to start learning and adapting. There were doors that needed to be broken down, and I think that groups like Soft Cell, Bronski Beat and Frankie Goes to Hollywood did break them down. It was the beginning of a movement that I think played a part in changing the attitudes of my generation.

Marc Almond: To say that there wasn't an enjoyable side to it all would be a lie. Ray Davies said, 'Success is revenge', and that certainly is true. Payback for the bullies and those that dismissed me because I wasn't good at school or academic.[22]

Annie Hogan: I do think they enjoyed it to begin with, girls screaming and chasing them down the street.[23]

Mike Wiand celebrated Soft Cell's success by inviting Dave Ball and his then girlfriend to accompany him to see the Four Tops as their nostalgia-based tour hit the nearby town of Batley. Accompanying the quartet on a night out in Sheffield afterwards, Ball was mortified when the DJ at local nightclub Maximillions stopped the music, introduced 'Dave Ball of Soft Cell' over the PA and played 'Tainted Love', all the while entirely ignoring the Motown legends. Shortly afterwards Ball was also invited for a drink with 'Tainted Love' writer Ed Cobb at the Old Selfridges Hotel; perhaps in anticipation of the many millions in royalties the cover was to earn him, Cobb bought all the drinks. They would meet again two years later during Soft Cell's sold-out residency at the Hollywood Palace, where the songwriter was distraught to hear they had stopped playing the track live, by now sick to death of its ubiquity.[24]

Stevo: I was once in the south of France and a bottle of champagne suddenly appeared on the table. The waiter said, 'It's from the gentleman in the corner.' Through my curiosity I walked over to see who they were. He said he was Ed Cobb.[25]

Beneath the wild emotional lurches brought on by sudden fame, however, a more insidious sense of unease was beginning to take root. How could Soft Cell square their new-found status as pop stars with the radical designs the band had sprung from? Could the band so inspired by the radical teachings of Jeff Nuttall and John Darling, the sonic assaults of Throbbing Gristle and Suicide, the darkness and grit of post-industrial Leeds and the aesthetics of sinister camp from Weimar Germany to the end of the pier, whose manager was an anarchic teenager, really continue to operate without compromise under these sudden new conditions? Ultimately, it would be the two opposing pulls – enormous fame and radical art – that would tear Soft Cell apart within just two and a half years.

Bedsit Land

Dave Ball: Our main aspiration had been to be a successful indie band. We'd have been quite happy to be in the indie charts. We'd never thought about the pop charts. It never crossed our minds.[26]

For now, however, Soft Cell's 'Tainted Love' success had earnt them enough credit with Phonogram to sign a full album deal, and to release an original as the single's much anticipated follow-up. They chose 'Bedsitter', another fixture of their live sets, a song inspired directly by the grotty environs they occupied in Leeds. Tim Pope, an unknown young director, managed to blag his way into filming a claustrophobic video, augmenting Almond's imagery through nauseous psychedelia.

Tim Pope, music video director: I'd never made any videos before 'Bedsitter'. I was storyboarding loads of songs, but people were telling me, 'But you haven't made a video'. I went to the Phonogram office where this rather nervous, shivering person, dressed in black with bare white arms came in. I remember sitting with Marc, playing 'Bedsitter' while I told loads of lies about things that I'd done and sold him the idea. I was very aware that they were a big cheese and I was nothing, but Marc and I immediately connected with our shared underground leanings. I loved the song's themes, it reminded me of films like *Room at the Top*, so I came up with this idea of Marc, trapped in this place as if forever. I came up with this idea of Marc's shirts matching the wallpaper, so he disappeared into the apartment and became one with it.[27]

Josephine Warden: When I hear that song, I hear Marc and I with no money. I can relate to it. He captured that time. His lyrics are poetry to me, poetry about how were living – with no money![28]

Dave Ball: Once we got the album deal, Mike said, 'Do you want to come over to New York and do it there?' We could get away from the pressure of London and being recognised, being the new pop sensations and such nonsense. We agreed the next single was going to be 'Bedsitter'. Recording it was quite intense, and it was made worse because the record company from London phoned up and said, 'You're still number one in Germany, they want you to do a TV show in Dusseldorf and you'll be number one for another week, it'll mean another twenty-five thousand sales.' I was like, 'We're trying to get the bloody follow-up single!' Marc had the idea – he had this friend back in Leeds who was tall with dark hair. He said, 'He can fly with me to Dusseldorf and just stand behind the keyboard.' No one knew what I looked like, all the focus was on Marc, so they went off to Dusseldorf and the record stayed at number one in Germany. I managed to finish 'Bedsitter', and no one was any the wiser.[29]

Marc Almond: 'Bedsitter' was an obvious choice, one of Soft Cell's best songs along with 'Torch' and 'Say Hello, Wave Goodbye'. A perfect record.[30]

Dave Ball: I prefer 'Bedsitter' to 'Tainted Love'. The subject matter actually means something. 'Tainted Love' has very mediocre lyrics; it was only the B-side of a flop record when Gloria Jones did it![31]

Phonogram, however, saw 'Bedsitter' differently. With its synths that swirl like a hungover head and its lyrics about a crash back to a hungry, empty, cold, boring reality after the cheap happiness of a night out, 'Bedsitter' was not what they had in mind: an upbeat song about the night before, rather than a kitchen-sink vignette about the morning after.

Dave Ball: They wanted something more simple. 'Tainted Love' is such a basic, obvious pop song – it just repeats the same four notes over and over – but 'Bedsitter' is not quite so obvious. When we finished the record, we had to send the tape over on a jet from New York to London. The phone goes a couple of days later: 'We don't think it's good enough.' Me and Marc are suddenly seeing our entire promising career disappear before our eyes. I was furious, and Marc went into this massive depression; he just disappeared. A couple of days later he returned with this woman called Cindy Ecstasy. His mood had changed; I think her surname could give you a clue as to why.[32]

Chapter 7

I SHOOK THEM UP AND I GAVE THEM HELL

Marc Almond had in fact already met Cindy Ecstasy on his first night in New York. Word had travelled fast that the architects of 'Tainted Love' (as well as 'Memorabilia', whose success in the US clubs had rescued Soft Cell's record deal in the first place) were in town, and he had been invited on a night out at Studio 54 by promoter Jim Fouratt. Plied with more drugs than he could handle, he collapsed on the dance floor before he was rescued by a group of mysterious and beautiful women. A few nights later, at an after-hours club called Berlin, he bumped into one of them again, with whom he struck up an immediate friendship. The day after that she called him up and invited him to her apartment in Brooklyn, where, with the Cure's 'All Cats Are Grey' from the album *Faith* playing on her record player, she introduced him to a pill that few at that time had access to.

Ecstasy was legal in America until 1985, but was at that point still extremely rare outside of medical circles, in which the psychologist Leo Zeff was waxing lyrical about its therapeutic potential, recommending it to doctors across the country who then did the same. Cindy's supply was therefore medical grade, and all but unknown among non-doctors back in Britain.[1]

Brian Moss: Marc came back to Leeds briefly and brought some back with him on the plane. He told us all about this legal drug called ecstasy. He said it feels amazing and you don't get a comedown, if you drink some coffee, it brings you up, but avoid alcohol. People in Leeds had never heard of it. There were only two chemists in New York doing it, I think.

Annie Hogan: Marc was suddenly all, 'Honey, I love you!' Like, what the hell? Marc was never like that with me. He was normally more like my big brother. I didn't want anything to do with ecstasy for ages![2]

Dave Ball: Prior to that we might have a bit of speed or something back in Leeds, the odd blue pill, maybe a bit of poppers. I didn't smoke cannabis and we couldn't afford cocaine. When you've suddenly got money, then it all becomes available.[3]

Beverley Glick: I got a series of postcards from Marc, addressed to Betty Page, c/o *Sounds*, London, that would somehow find their way to me. When they first went out there, I got one from New York, saying, 'My God, you won't believe it, it's just so brilliant, so exciting here. You must come!'

Cindy would end up being one of the most pivotal – if mysterious – supporting players as the band fast approached their peak, not only for her creative contributions as a singer, rapper and actor in their videos, but because of the drug from which she took her name, and the lifestyle that it would fuel – a dizzying and delirious party, soundtracked by the world's greatest dance music pummelling through the world's best sound systems. It would come to define their lives as they recorded *Non-Stop Erotic Cabaret*.

After being flown out to New York first class, Soft Cell were picked up by a stretch Cadillac and driven to an apartment owned by the studio Mediasound on the Upper West Side of Manhattan.

Dave Ball: We'd get a yellow taxi to the studio at about ten in the morning, have breakfast, then start work at about eleven. We'd be finished by about six, so we probably only did about seven hours a day, five days a week. We had the evenings and weekends to ourselves. That was where the fun began.[4]

Mike Thorne: They tore into the club scene with total gusto. That was quite nice to see. The 1980s were a fantastic time to be in New York. The club scene was vibrant, there were so many ideas flashing around and so much talent. A typical week for me would be two pm until midnight in the studio, then checking out bands until three.[5]

It was not long until Vicious Pink were flown out to join the sessions at Mediasound – a functional, high-tech space on the site of a former church. As backing singers they had stayed one step removed from the explosion that greeted 'Tainted Love', and so the juxtaposition between New York and Leeds was stark.

Josephine Warden: Put it this way, one week I was walking home from the poly because I'd spent all my money on a packet of fags. The next I was on a first-class flight to New York, staying in a fabulous apartment on the Upper West Side. And the drugs were legal. It's the only place I've ever got a culture shock. I got out of the car from the airport, I was standing on a busy street, and it was about five o'clock in the morning. Just the noise, the speed and the buzz of New York even then, it was like, 'What the fuck is going on here?'[6]

Brian Moss: Marc had been there and come back, Dave was already over there, so we flew over with Marc and Stevo. When we landed at JFK airport, Jose [Warden] and Marc went to get some money changed and a girl came up to me and said, 'Do you want a lift?' I was a bit apprehensive, but she told us how she would wait at the airport, looking for people who looked like they were in a band. She drove us to Manhattan and dropped us off and we arranged to meet her later that evening. Now we were on a busy street in the dark, carrying our suitcases and trying to hail a cab, with two guys near us punching moving cabs that weren't stopping for them. We crossed the road, then managed to hail a cab, to our relief, straight to the apartment.

The apartment was nice, with a very 1970s décor. It had a TV with twenty-six channels, wow! We only had BBC1, BBC2 and Yorkshire Television back home, and those three ended at midnight. Later that evening we all took ecstasy and headed to [the bar] Pete's Place, where our new friend recommended we meet up. We ended up walking down all these dark deserted alleys, like those old black and white gangster movies, with metal trash cans strewn about.

I shook them up and I gave them hell

Stevo: There was a gunshot on the corner of the block. We all jumped. Marc and Dave just wanted to get home. But after a few days that all changed. Soft Cell fell in love with New York.[7]

Marc Almond: There were the drugs, of course, and amazing creative people, dance music like I'd never heard before. It was a totally wild and vibrant time to be there in New York. I felt at home for the first time.[8]

Along with Cindy, Soft Cell and their friends soon formed a circle of socialites and scenesters, within which Almond and Ball then established inner circles of their own – Almond's crew included a Marilyn Monroe lookalike called Jane, a top-less dancer called Elise, a photographer called Skipper and the dominatrix and writer Mistress Angel Stern, aka Terence Sellers.

Harvey Goldberg, Mediasound engineer: It's funny, they would both go out and hit the same spots, but with two different crowds. Some of it might have been that Marc was gay and Dave was heterosexual, and some of it might have been that although they were both party animals, Dave was a bit more low key about it than Marc.[9]

Beverley Glick: Because of 'Tainted Love', every door was open to them, everybody wanted to host them and invite them into their clubs. The first time I flew out it was a complete thrill ride from beginning to end. And obviously that was my first experience of ecstasy because they wanted all their friends to take it as well. There were lots of nights out that I think back to now and I have to question whether they actually happened, like when Marc introduced us to a dominatrix friend of his and we went out clubbing with her apprentices, or when he took us to the Anvil; I'd never been to a heavy-duty S&M club before – it was just mad! One thing about Marc is that he wanted to share his success with his friends, and if you were in his inner circle, he was extremely generous.

Dianne Brill, New York club kid: They were stars with a huge hit, and such fucking cool people that immediately, everyone wanted them in the room. We loved the art that they produced and we wanted to bring them into the fold. Marc was full of curiosity, always wanting to know 'What's this? What's that?', and that childlike curiosity was very New York.[10]

Don Wershba, Mediasound engineer: Anyone who comes to New York for the first time is awed by it, but the thing that was so admirable about Marc and Dave was that they weren't intimidated. Some are scared, and others are just like, 'Bring it on'. New York was this mass of energy, and they took to it like a fish to water. They were fearless in that regard. Dave was much quieter about it – butter wouldn't melt in his mouth – and Marc was more demonstrative, but both of them made friends everywhere they went.[11]

Dianne Brill: Our punk scene was not as deeply rooted [as in Britain] and shifted very quickly into new wave and a more inclusive vibe. In England it was a groovy thing to say, 'I'm bored, I'm bored, I'm bored', like Eeyore, whereas over here we were a little bit more Tigger. I think as soon as the Brits came to Tigger territory, they'd all be Tigger too. We acted jaded, we'd stand against the wall, smoke a cigarette and try to act cool, but inside I think all these artists just wanted to be included and really express everything, every little thought. We always liked new people, and of course all the girls were thrilled by all these gorgeous British guys with their whole vibe and style coming into the club.

The previous decade is often considered to have marked a period of intense decline for New York in the wake of the USA's first post-war recession from 1973 until 1975, where public services deteriorated as crime rose. In the wider country, the swagger of the 1960s had by now given way to a national psyche pocked by Watergate, the murder of Civil Rights figureheads and military defeat in Vietnam.[12] There was a reason that the American soul scene had long since departed the up-tempo thrills the Northern Soul crew were still so enamoured by.

Harvey Goldberg: New York was going through an interesting phase during that period. It was coming out of a period of economic depression, it had already turned the corner by the time they got here, but there was still a lot of it that was seedy.

Jack Fritscher, author and social activist: New York was a flaming trash bin of danger and crime. Spend half an hour looking at Scorsese's *Mean Streets* to get an idea what it was like.[13]

Richard Boch, doorman at the Mudd Club: It was very rough, and not as crowded as it is today. SoHo was deserted in the evenings; now it's bumper-to-bumper traffic.[14]

In 1979, Gallup pollsters found just 19 per cent of Americans were satisfied with the way things were going in their country, with public trust in the government at 29 per cent. By the following spring, trust had slipped to 25 per cent.[15] Through it all, however, nightlife had thrived. In the same way the New Romantics and Blitz Kids in Leeds and London intensified the vibrancy of their creative pursuits by contrasting them with the dourness of the world outside, so too did party-goers in New York. Foremost among the clubs was Studio 54, which opened in 1976 and soon emerged as the nucleus of a disco craze that went international – in part thanks to the success of *Saturday Night Fever* the following year.[16] An upside of the national recession meanwhile was cheap rent for a generation of musicians, artists, clubbers and self-promoters for whom the risks of city life were more than worth taking. The situation was only boosted further by the emergence of spaces newly vacated thanks to deindustrialisation and the movement of the middle classes to the suburbs. So cheap was the rent that, eventually, some landlords began to realise that they could earn more money by illicitly burning down their decrepit properties and claiming insurance money than they could from tenants. The apartments left un-burnt were often grim, but for many that was merely an excuse to spend more time in the thriving clubland outside.

Pamina Brassey, New York clubber: It was dangerous. But when you're a teenager, you feel impervious to crime. You feel immortal. There was a certain energy in New York that anyone who went there would have felt. People went there to pursue their dreams and their arts. Everywhere you looked people were making music or films.[17]

I shook them up and I gave them hell

Rudolf Piper, owner, Danceteria nightclub: Our whole building was thirteen floors; I think the lease was six grand a month. Nowadays you'd only get a small apartment for that.[18]

Richard Boch: I thought I was really pushing the envelope by moving into a loft that I was sharing with someone and renting for $400 a month. Before that I was sharing an apartment on Bleecker Street that was $175 a month and had a bathtub in the kitchen. You put a board on top of it and it would become part of your kitchen counter.

Pamina Brassey: It was cheap! It was dingy, you know. If you went to CBGB you're on the same street where the drunks polish your windshields and ask for quarters, but that didn't phase us. There were galleries happening everywhere, people selling art out of an ice cream van or something. It was exciting.

By the time Almond met Ecstasy at Studio 54, the legendary disco was starting to wane following a turbulent period of licensing issues, accusations of profit-skimming, tax evasion, party favours and a change of ownership in 1981, but it was still a force.[19] Elsewhere were a host of other clubs, each with its entirely distinct personality.

Rudolf Piper: A club at that time had to have a certain philosophy. It had to have a point of view. One used to judge a person by the nightclub this person went to. In Studio 54, of course, you were fabulous. If this person went to Xenon, they're probably Eurotrash. If this person went to Club A, they were an uptown Donald Trump type.

Harvey Goldberg: New York from the mid-1970s to the mid-1980s was really like the club capital of the world, the centre of the universe for nightlife. There may have been one or two clubs in Paris, or one or two clubs in London that were important, LA I don't even think was on the map at that point, but New York had easily fifteen clubs a night that would have been the place to be. Music was so intertwined into street life in New York. It wasn't even the 'cool' factor of it, it wasn't about being seen, it was just that you left feeling like you had been invited to the best party that had been going on that night. And at the same time that's going on in the dance clubs we had CBGB, which was one of the most important springboards for a band to play.

When Soft Cell arrived, CBGB was still riding high on its role as a launchpad for the stars of new wave like Blondie, Television and Talking Heads in the late 1970s.[20] The Ritz had recently followed in its wake, opening up in Webster Hall in 1980 as the first venue in the world to incorporate live video. That same year had seen the relaunch of the Peppermint Lounge – where the world-wide craze for the twist had begun in the 1960s – at the site of what had previously been the gay bar GG's Barnum Room.

Pamina Brassey: GG Barnum's [sic] was the transvestite disco and it was tremendous fun. Three floors of swinging disco baths, $5 to get in and you got two cocktails. I had my first experience seeing Puerto Rican hustlers, and there were ballet dancers from the New York City Ballet.

I shook them up and I gave them hell

The importance of New York's pre-AIDS LGBTQ+ scene – much of which centred around Christopher Street in the West Village – when it came to providing much of the city's energy is impossible to understate.

Jack Fritscher: The Vietnam War did not end until 1975, so gay men were still being recruited off the streets to die. A lot of us were also war babies, conceived before, during and just after World War Two. We knew that there had been camps set up to put 'enemies of the state' in, and we figured that those camps would be opened up again for us because of the attacks on gay people that had culminated in the late 1970s with the moral majority, Anita Bryant and Jerry Falwell. We were bringing that PTSD into the clubs. The politics in the streets washed right into the club scene. What people felt with passion in the streets, they felt in the clubs.

Dianne Brill: It was good to be gay in New York, but idiots would still come and cause trouble in areas where they were hanging out. Christopher Street in the West Village, even in the daytime there would be assaults and stuff like that.

In part, the gay scene's success was also thanks to the mafia's role in running many of the venues – ownership that was more permissive towards queer patrons, as long as they paid their protection money on time.

Jack Fritscher: Remember, the raid on Stonewall originally happened over taxes more than anything else. Marc Almond would have been free to be himself partly because of that mafia embrace, which then had another, interior embrace by the gay crowd looking out for the gay crowd. Hermetically sealed between these two embraces it was a womb-like atmosphere, where they could have developed their foetal ideas about themselves.

At the more forward-thinking clubs, DJs and bookers were also beginning to embrace hip hop, which had already been thriving in the Bronx since the early 1970s. There, DJ Kool Herc had been the first to spot young dancers' obsession with 'breaks' – a jazz term for the moments where drummers could cut loose while the rest of the band held back – and to experiment with simply playing one break after another, crudely fading between each one, during one of the block parties he had organised with his sister Cindy Campbell. The virtuosic Grandmaster Flash refined the art of mixing, Grand Wizzard Theodore put Flash's ideas of record scratching to practice, while Afrika Bambaataa had introduced extraordinary eclecticism – his sets veering from Hare Krishna chants and TV themes, to Gary Numan and an isolated Ringo Starr drum part from *Sgt. Pepper's Lonely Hearts Club Band*.[21]

Hip hop's spread from the Bronx and Harlem was gradual but significant. Fab 5 Freddy's efforts to get graffiti (one of hip hop's four pillars along with DJing, MCing and break-dancing) recognised by the 'serious' New York art crowd, and his collaboration with filmmaker Charlie Ahearn to produce the first hip hop motion picture, *Wild Style*, were pivotal. So too was his introduction of twenty-one-year-old Englishwoman Ruza Blue to the world of roller-skating – a fad then so cool that venues like the Ritz were as fashionable and cutting-edge as Studio 54.[22]

I shook them up and I gave them hell

New York Times, 20 March 1981: Somehow, the stroke-stroke of roller skating seems perfectly suited to the bamp-bamp-bamp of disco [...] Most skaters agree that the Roxy is to roller skating what Studio 54 was to disco. Its cavernous interior even looks a bit like Studio 54: the complex light system in hot reds and cool blues, the silver skyline along the back wall and the red velvet ropes outside bespeaking exclusivity.[23]

Ruza Blue: I loved what Rusty Egan was doing at the Blitz Club in London and I wanted to do something with fashion and music but with NY 'flava'.[24]

Blue met Freddy at a Bow Wow Wow show in 1981, attending on the advice of her then boss Malcolm McLaren (himself to make a major, if controversial, step into hip hop with his *Duck Rock* LP a few years later). There, she was blown away by the night's support act, Afrika Bambaataa. Before long, she had started a night of her own at a tiny East Village club called Negril. After being evicted when it was discovered her overcrowded parties were violating fire department regulations, she spent a short time at Danceteria, and took over a run-down roller rink at the Roxy for a night she called 'Wheels of Steel', where she would invite rockers like the Clash to DJ as well as the rising stars of hip hop in an effort to bring the culture of the latter into the mainstream.[25]

Ruza Blue: The events I produced at Roxy were different and original because of the mash-up entertainment and the hip hop elements working together in an electronic dance music environment, and also where the concept of mixing up as many cultures, music, art, dance, fashion scenes and styles and people was possible. If it fit, I would put it in the mix. You could only experience this vibe at the Roxy; no one else was doing it and we had the hippest cross-cultural crowd New York City had ever seen before. Everyone who was anyone was at the Roxy on a Friday night; it was the only place to be in New York City.[26]

Dave Ball: I saw loads of hip hop at the Roxy roller disco like Funky 4 + 1 and Grandmaster Flash. Hip hop was this mature, joined-up-at-the-edges culture. There was the graffiti, the dress code; it wasn't just the records. The whole thing was full-on. Britain was only just starting to get into that kind of stuff. New York was about ten years ahead in terms of music and culture.[27]

Just as the birth of independent music culture had allowed Soft Cell to release the *Mutant Moments* EP, so too did it herald a plethora of releases from New Yorkers who would hitherto have had no way of getting their music heard. ZE Records rose out of former Velvet Underground member John Cale and his partner (and Patti Smith's manager) Jane Friedman's SPY imprint, and quickly established itself as one of the most fashionable labels on earth thanks to a roster stuffed with rising New York talent.[28] Meanwhile, 99 Records grew from a clothing store in Greenwich Village to provide a home for no wave heroes Glenn Branca and Bush Tetras, as well as genre-flipping pioneers ESG.[29] Underground rock and reggae also found a home on ROIR, which began as a cassette-only imprint in 1979 in an effort to capitalise on the launch of the Sony Walkman the same year, and later released Television, Suicide and the New York Dolls.[30]

Aside from widely circulated bootleg cassettes of DJs' mixes, hip hop culture made its own inroads on vinyl when Harlem businessman Paul Winley resurrected his Winley Records imprint – initially a doo-wop label in the 1950s – first to release select speeches by Malcolm X, then the first breakbeat compilation, and then two of the first proper hip hop singles in 'Rhymin' and Rappin'' by his teenaged daughters Tanya and Paulette in 1979 and 'Vicious Rap' by Tanya, aka Sweet Tee, the following year. Another Harlemite, veteran record seller Bobby Robinson, revived his own label Enjoy to allow Grandmaster Flash to enter the fray with 'Superrappin' the same year, while husband-and-wife duo Sylvia and Joe Robinson formed Sugarhill Records and manufactured the group the Sugarhill Gang, whose 'Rapper's Delight' became the first hip hop song to break the top forty.[31]

Genre boundaries were blurring, too. Even at the much larger Chrysalis Records, new wave outliers Blondie were constantly hopping between punk, disco and rap. 'Rapture' (1980) would be the first song featuring rap vocals to reach number one, namechecking Fab 5 Freddy in reflection of his introducing Debbie Harry to the pivotal Bronx hip hop club Disco Fever. Grandmaster Flash had been slated to appear as a DJ in the video, but after going AWOL on the day of filming was replaced last minute by Jean-Michel Basquiat.

As a result of this explosion in diverse, boundary-pushing music, the city's DJs found themselves presented with a hitherto unseen breadth of options when it came to the music they could play, from across New York's diverse musical spectrum. All of this made the soundtrack to the New York night thrilling in its diversity. A DJ at the short-lived but highly influential Mudd Club, for instance, could pivot in an instant from funk to punk to new wave to no wave, to the kind of electronic weirdness that Stevo had been playing in London.

Pamina Brassey: We loved 'Warm Leatherette' by the Normal. Those British weirdos were very appealing to the people downtown.

The Mudd Club had set itself up as the shadowy, under-ground opposite of Studio 54's burst of glamour. It was the anti-disco, a narrow loft space named in tribute to the doctor Samuel Alexander Mudd, who became a pariah when he honoured his Hippocratic oath to treat President Lincoln's assassin, John Wilkes Booth. Instead of the velvet rope across the door at Studio 54, they opted for a metal chain.[32] An electric gate at one end of the room would roll away to reveal the night's performers – whether the B-52s or Frank Zappa. It was perhaps the most forward-thinking club of all; their DJ Johnny Dynell even tried to initiate a col-laboration between Suicide and Grandmaster Flash, after being stunned by Flash's dexterity on the decks one night in 1979.[33]

Richard Boch: The Mudd Club was incredibly nondescript. It was on a nondescript block in a nondescript neighbourhood. What made the Mudd Club the Mudd Club was what went on inside, the people who showed up. It wasn't all about being beautiful and dressed up, it was 'Were you an artist?' Were you Richard Serra in a dirty t-shirt, Robert Rauschenberg drunk getting out of a cab? Were you Brice Marden, an incredibly handsome, up and coming artist, or Jean-Michel Basquiat with a can of spray paint, painting the bathrooms and getting thrown out? What made you interesting enough to come in? That was the core of what the Mudd Club was about – a multi-disciplinary gaggle.

None would be more important in the Mudd Club scene than Anita Sarko, with whom Almond struck up a firm friendship, and Ball a romantic relationship. A Detroit-born psychology graduate from Michigan State University, she arrived in New York in 1979. On her first night out, the Mudd Club's door-man deemed her too uncool to enter. She snuck in nonethe-less, and within a month was helming the DJ booth in the club's VIP room.[34]

Richard Boch: She dressed well, she was fearless, she always looked good. She really pursued that job, sneaking in, drop-ping off tapes for [owner] Steve Mass to listen to, prodding him into giving her an opportunity to spin one night. I don't think he actually showed up, but then told her that she was hired.

Other than at gay clubs, New York DJs were usually male, but Sarko was a pioneer not only in terms of gender but taste. As well as offbeat funk, proto electronica and obscure oldies, she was one of the first to play early hip hop records by Kurtis Blow and Sugar Hill Gang to the downtown sce-nesters. One night, a long set of African music proved so divisive that she was pelted with ashtrays.[35]

Richard Boch: She could be into noise as music, or metal as music. She could be into a Lou Reed ballad, or a 'Tainted Love' remix. She had a record collection that was kind of unrivalled.

Dave Ball: Anita and I used to have heated arguments. She'd say that DJs were artists, just as important as musicians. I'd say, 'No, they're not, they're just playing what other people have written', but now I agree with her. Back then, they really were artists. They would pick out stuff I'd never heard before, and the quality of mixing was the best I'd ever heard. They could make one track last an hour but dip in and out of loads of other tracks at the same time. It was absolutely brilliant.[36]

Dianne Brill: I became connected with Soft Cell through Anita. My God, how do you describe that woman. I've never met anyone like her before or since. She was the first important female DJ that I ever heard of, and she had the intelligence that people who are so smart they're funny have. She was sardonic, which Marc loved, of course. She had her 'hate club' and she'd always have someone she despised to talk about intensely, but she really brought something out in all of us. I think there was a gentleness about her talent. She was a powerhouse goddess. I think she would have been a real inspiration to Soft Cell in so many ways.

Placed on the guest list wherever they pleased, Almond, Ball, Sarko, Ecstasy and their friends sampled all these flavours of the New York night, often hiring a limousine for their nights out because it was cheaper between them than a taxi.

I shook them up and I gave them hell

Brian Moss: Cindy Ecstasy wasn't a drug dealer because it wasn't illegal. She was more like our guide who took us to all the cool places. We'd go to all the clubs, get looked after. The Warehouse had been the only club like it in Leeds. In most cities in the UK there was only one cool club, but in New York you could just go from one to another to another. In the UK it was 2 a.m., then that was it, but in New York one club would open 'til 2 a.m., then another would open from two 'til the early hours of the morning. In one, I think it was called Berlin, we met Billy Idol and spent all night with him and got breakfast together at ten the next morning.

Pamina Brassey: There were clubs, then there were after-hours clubs, then there were after-after-hours clubs, then people would go to the Empire Diner for breakfast. You could keep going for days in New York if you wanted to. When I first went to London, I found it really hard to find any equivalent.

Josephine Warden: New York was hedonistic at that time, just absolutely crazy. There was a lot of cocaine about, a lot of ecstasy about. Some people had a whole lot of money, and the people who didn't used to dress up as glamorous as anyone that did. We were in the right place at the right time.[37]

Pamina Brassey: After a certain time, people become a bit more OTT, you know? Heavier on the drugs. The crazies came out downtown. I remember seeing people dancing on broken glass. There were some people that never saw the light of day; they were just clubbing people who slept all day.

Jack Fritscher: At places like Studio 54 everyone was all together, straight men held back a bit but gay men did not hold back from straight men. In the tradition of *Cabaret*, it was customary for gay men to be a walker for the women, or to have a woman on his arm, and it was all mixed on the dancefloor. But then it was like the clock striking midnight in the Cinderella story – every mouse ran off to its proper little den. There were after-hours places for straight people, and there were after-hours places for gay people.

Almond was particularly fascinated with the Meatpacking District, around which the city's sex clubs, trans spaces and burgeoning BDSM subculture had begun to revolve. It had risen up in the spaces left vacant as the meat industry slowly declined and was all but anonymous from the outside. Under mafia control or police protection rackets, illegal prostitution and drug dealing also flourished. To Almond, a writer increasingly interested in the world's illicit and seedy underbellies, the district and its clubs like Hellfire (the most heterosexual-friendly in the BDSM scene), the Anvil and the Manhole were a source of inspiration. Most infamous of all was the hyper-exclusive Mineshaft, established by former theatre man Wally Wallace in the site of a former disco of the same name, and featuring a bathtub that acquired legendary status, having been moved across the country after being salvaged from San Francisco bathhouse the Barracks following a fire.[38]

Jack Fritscher: The area was deserted at night, apart from the butchers in their aprons, carrying bloody carcasses of dead meat from refrigerated trucks sitting there idling. They'd ignore you completely as they walked past, carrying the carcasses over their shoulders and hanging them on hooks – which wasn't that much different to what was going on once you got inside the Mineshaft. If you as an individual had walked in, pretty soon one or two men might have picked up on you, and then other voyeurs, and then pretty soon a whole orgy would have developed around you to which you were nuclear. It was amniotic in a sense, like being in the womb and being one of the million sperm your father had just ejaculated trying to make it to the egg, the moment of triumph. There was also access to the roof. It was absolutely gorgeous to have sex there, all the city lit up around you. Even then, we knew that nothing that wonderful could last forever. On Fourth of July they might be grilling hot dogs – you could have an all-American hot-dog picnic on the roof, then go down and throw it up on somebody who wanted it. Nothing like a warmed-over meal!

Anybody with theatre chops would recognise Wally's theatre background and the way he created the sound stage of the Mineshaft. In the play areas, except for the moaning, yelling and cheering it was mainly silent because everybody was grooving like this mass amoeba, three layers of men peeling and peeling off, while moving around in the bathtub was a guy lying in six gallons of piss and screed. At the same time there was a bass throbbing, because sex needs a rhythm. It wasn't a disco beat; it was a sex beat. Wally didn't want that disco energy in there because that was too frantic. The purpose wasn't to dance alone, it was to be as tribal as possible with another person or a group of people.

As a group, however, the Soft Cell crowd gravitated most to Danceteria, which had been opened by Jim Fouratt and German expatriate Rudolf Piper. Here the multi-genre, multi-disciplinary sensory overload of New York reached entirely new heights. A normal night would see performances from two live bands, two DJs manning the decks at any one time, an entire floor dedicated to experimental film and another to contemporary art.

Rudolf Piper: Initially, we had four floors, then we added a rooftop on the thirteenth floor. All the others between were empty. All the floors were adapted to different tastes. The first floor was where bands played; we presented bands seven nights a week. The second floor was for DJs and dancing, and the third floor was the first video lounge in New York – as well as a restaurant and bar. The fourth floor was an art exhibition space, geared towards French comic book art – they were quite intelligent, not superheroes and shit like that. The roof opened in the summer and there was always a great party to open the rooftop season and then to close it in September. The idea was that a person could migrate from floor to floor. There was discovery. There were also plenty of dark corners to do … things. You can guess what kind. *Non-Stop Erotic Cabaret* sort of things!

Dave Ball: For a couple of years it was the best club in New York. A totally different world.[39]

Rudolf Piper: At that time, British bands were all the rage. I had a talent agent in London and I went there myself many times to look for bands that were happening. There was a lot of talent in New York of course, and Danceteria presented it all, but the big thing was to bring British bands in for their debut in America.

Dianne Brill: Danceteria was the centre temple, where you could go any night of the week. Except the weekends, because then the bridge and tunnel people would come in and you didn't want to see them so much.

Rudolf Piper: At Danceteria you had to be a certain way. 'New wave' would be the best way to define it. There was a certain way to dress, a certain way to behave, a certain music. Keith Haring, Basquiat, etc. They were all orbiting around Danceteria.

Though Soft Cell's sudden lurch to fame in Britain had brought a mixture of petty jealousies, hangers-on and an uncomfortable relationship with a now-clamouring press, in New York their fame's main advantage was allowing additional scope for them to melt away into the delirium.

Dave Ball: Everyone was cooler. They'll know who you are, but they won't be gushing, going crazy, saying 'Can I have your autograph?'[40]

Rudolf Piper: In Studio 54, celebrities like Elizabeth Taylor could arrive without security. They had a certain hour for the paparazzi to take photographs, and if a photographer took a photo that was considered inconvenient, he was barred from coming into the club again. There was a lot of coke and fucking going on those upper floors, but very few photos of it.

In Danceteria, paparazzi were not allowed at all, and taking a photo of yourself – 'look at me, I'm at the club' – was considered so uncool. The only person allowed to take photos in the club was Andy Warhol.

Dave Ball: I once asked Jim Fouratt, who seemed to know everyone, 'Do you know Andy?' He said, 'Sure, do you want to meet him?' We got an appointment to go to the factory and he was exactly what I expected. Very blank. 'Gee, wow', and a really limp handshake. He started taking pictures of us and recording our voices, so I took the liberty of getting my Instamatic out; he didn't seem to mind. It lasted about an hour. I see it as one of our great achievements, really.[41]

Marc Almond: The whole New York art scene had an incredible influence on us. We were taken to meet Warhol, one of my heroes; the nightclubs were of the like I'd never been to. I felt at home for the first time. Of course, that found its way into the studio. Our first two albums are infused with that energy.[42]

The Mediasound studio was a place of relative stillness compared to the blooming, buzzing confusion outside. Conscious of the scale of the opportunity on offer to them, they took the sessions seriously, avoiding the prolific drug-taking that was defining their lives outside.

Don Wershba: If they were doing recreational substances, it was definitely not during the sessions. It was worktime; there was no fucking about. Mike [Thorne] had this theory that there are only five or six creative hours in the day, and we really got a lot done. The sessions were very efficient. I don't remember people showing up late, or running off to the bathroom.

Soft Cell's lyrics had been written about Leeds and London, Blackpool and Southport, and identikit towns just like them across their home country, teasing out scenes from the dark, silly, sleazy otherworld that slithered and squirmed under the surface of everyday British banality. They recorded them, however, in a state of buzzing whiplash from New York's altogether more intense nights out, the former filtering through the latter and imbibing an American melodrama in the process. Their songs took on flourishes of the city's soundtrack, from the pummel of the disco beat to the experimentation of no wave to the dynamic momentum of hip hop.

Don Wershba: One day they came in and said, 'Oh, we were at this club last night and we heard the most amazing thing! Mike, you're gonna have to make this sound for us on your synthesiser. They put these records on and were rotating them backwards and forwards more and more rapidly.' It was the first anybody had heard of scratching. Mike thought about it and came up with some crazy way of emulating it.

In Mike Thorne they had the perfect producer to tease this out. His process was not passive as much as it was chameleonic, shifting to accommodate whatever the band wanted to bring. His demeanour was calm and his breadth of knowledge considerable. He was a stable presence at which Soft Cell could throw everything they were picking up on their nights out.

145

Mike Thorne: In my case, I never did drink and drugs in the studio because I have to keep a square head on to judge people's emotional output. Weekends are a different matter entirely. You often hear fancy production, but it's always been my aim to remove the barriers between the performers and the listener. I would try to draw on absolutely nothing [in terms of influences].[43]

Don Wershba: He was kind of the anchor, plus he had this tremendous knowledge of technology and synthesisers. I learnt a lot from Mike, I'll put it that way. It was a combination of having something prepared, but then also leaving a lot of room for the unknown, happy mistakes and happy accidents. When you were in the studio with Mike it wasn't going to get out of control, but it was still going to be a lot of fun, it was still going to be creative.

For some of those working in Mediasound, whose personal interests and previous clients had been old-school rock and roll, there was to be a culture shock of their own – particularly when it came to Soft Cell's sense of humour and the altogether more joyous kind of hedonism they were embarking on.

Harvey Goldberg: I was used to the rock and roll party life and seeing it in the studio – I had done some work with Keith Richards before working with Soft Cell – but this had a different energy to it. That whole genre of musicians didn't take themselves as seriously, so there was a lighter feel to the debauchery of the time than there would have been with rock and roll.

I shook them up and I gave them hell

Don Wershba: 'Sex Dwarf', that was one of the funniest sessions. I'm just looking at Mike and Mike's looking at me saying, 'This is just nuts'. But then there's 'Say Hello, Wave Goodbye', just a beautiful, beautiful song. It hadn't been my kind of music before, I was into rock and roll, live bands with drummers and bass players, the Who, the Stones, Led Zeppelin. But though Marc was not like a traditional singer, there were moments where it's like, 'Holy fuck, that's really, really special'.

Brian Moss: There were always good vibrations. Everybody who worked on it was just really nice. The studio was amazing. I think it all comes out in the recording; it's almost party-like and we had so much fun. I was the voice of the 'Sex Dwarf'. On other songs, Josephine and I sang together, apart from 'Seedy Films' where Jose did a wonderful silky-smooth solo vocal. All this non-stop fun, from the clubbing, the ecstasy, the people we met, the wonderful city that wasn't as scary as we were made to believe, all made it onto the atmosphere of the recording.

Josephine Warden: The good thing about ecstasy in those days was that you could just get a couple of hours sleep and then go into the studios and work. We were probably still buzzing. I think you can hear that party atmosphere. I still hear that energy when I listen to the album now.[44]

Harvey Goldberg: I know the record company didn't really understand why they didn't want to use real drums, not realising that they were literally the pioneers of where it was about to go. To me, it's always fun to work on something that then goes way beyond what you were doing in that room, I've been fortunate in my career many times to have wound up in the room for things that ended up being game changers, but we were just trying to have fun.

At the same time, however, Thorne's sense of distance – integral as it was to allowing *Non-Stop Erotic Cabaret* the room to breathe – was beginning to elicit a tension that was only to build as their working relationship progressed. Soft Cell could only be reined in so far before their primal, exploratory urge started to kick in.

Harvey Goldberg: I think they were a little offended by Mike not wanting to go out with them at night, out to the clubs, and I think part of that was because they wanted him to be influenced by the same things that they were starting to be influenced by. They felt that he needed to see the actual scene to understand what they were trying to achieve. The other part of it is that it's a normal growing process I've seen with a lot of acts where, at some point, they eat their own!

A launch party was held for *Non-Stop Erotic Cabaret* at Danceteria when the album was finally released, on 27 November 1981. Dianne Brill – whom Andy Warhol had once dubbed the Queen of the Night – was hired to organ-ise it, and given licence to go big. They hired dominatrices, leather boys and sex workers, circus entertainers and a who's who of downtown New York's party scene.

Dave Ball: Basically, we'd done the place out like the album. We got a load of dancers and strippers to act out these raunchy sex scenes and rip each other's clothes off while the album played. It was a completely drug- and alcohol-fuelled night. Lots of the New York scenesters were out. I remember Mick Jones from the Clash coming up to me and saying he really liked our album – I was extremely pleased about that because I was a massive fan of the Clash. So that was quite an honour. I don't know if Andy was there himself, but a lot of the Warhol people were all there. Madonna, too, before she was famous, because she always used to dance there.[45]

Dianne Brill: That was a very hot party. Rudolf and I were saying, 'OK, we've got to get the vibe of Soft Cell across'. We really did feel transformed by the songs, they were like a movement that brought you into an area of cool that you'd never been to before. How do you not respect that? Everyone there felt cool just to be in the same room as them, and they were very integrated; they didn't act like they were in a separate section behind a piece of velvet rope. That shit didn't exist back then.

The press reaction to *Non-Stop Erotic Cabaret*, however, was rather more muted.

NME, 28 November 1981: 'Tainted Love' was perfect – the functionary textures of electro pop shaken and shaped to invoke the remorse of a forgotten juke box gem … Well, what else could two little love torn lads do? Not much, is the answer provided by 'Non-Stop Erotic Cabaret'.[46]

Melody Maker, 28 November 1981: All in all, 'Non-Stop Erotic Cabaret' contains some of the most dispassionate songs since 'Transformer', some of the cruellest criticism since vintage Zappa, and some of the most pathetic posturing since Queen.[47]

Marc Almond: The critical reaction to *Non-Stop* was pretty dismissive. It hurt, of course, but wasn't unexpected after Paul Morley had come to visit us in Leeds for our first ever interview with a major music paper and had trashed us in such a cruel way. It shocked and hurt me, but it hardened me up. I had to get cynical and toughen up quick. I always felt the music papers at that time were lads' mags, down on electronic music. 'They didn't have guitars and it's for gays.' There was a sneeriness laced with a not always obvious homophobia.[48]

Reaching number five in the British albums chart, with the single 'Say Hello, Wave Goodbye' hitting number three, sales were still positive enough to warrant a hastily produced follow-up, *Non-Stop Ecstatic Dancing*, on which the band dived fully into clubland by remixing several songs into DJ-oriented twelve-inch versions.

The Human League – temporarily rebranded the League Unlimited Orchestra – released a similar rework of their own 1981 smash-hit LP *Dare* in the form of the hugely successful *Love and Dancing* just a couple of weeks later, which reflected producer Martin Rushent's love of Grandmaster Flash's turntable wizardry.[49] Both albums were a product of what was now becoming a major upshift in demand for longer songs, as electronic pop music took on more and more of an influence from club culture, and a market emerged among young people desperate to bring some of that exotic energy into their homes.[50] Though Soft Cell had wanted their favourite New York DJs to take on remix duty, Phonogram baulked at the idea and enlisted Thorne.

Mike Thorne: The seven-inch was the radio version – there was an obsession that the seven-inch had to sound good on the radio. But the twelve-inch delivered a much more coherent dance experience. You could guide people through an eight-, nine- or ten-minute experience. Get them going, then let the dancefloor change around them. At that time, a lot of dance records were made by chopping up bits of the twelve-inch and extending it further and further, but I would always record the twelve-inch first, then chop out the seven-inch from that.[51]

Dave Ball: There was a rumour that the whole of *Non-Stop Erotic Cabaret* was done on ecstasy, which was absolute nonsense. That album was a totally drug-free affair. But with the remix album that was closer to the truth.[52]

Though *Ecstatic Dancing* was in many ways a marketing exercise for Phonogram – the album included a new Northern Soul cover, this time of Melinda Marx's 1965 song 'What', as well as the version of 'Where Did Our Love Go?' that had already been merged with 'Tainted Love' the previous year – parts of the record stand as Soft Cell's pinnacle, where the ferocious energy of New York was present in its fullest force. 'Chips on My Shoulder' and 'Sex Dwarf' were stretched out from seedy vignettes to bona fide floor fillers.

'Memorabilia', meanwhile, returned as something altogether new. The original Daniel Miller version had managed

Bedsit Land

to slip Soft Cell past the velvet rope and into the clubs, but the *Ecstatic Dancing* version was the sound of the band now hyper-charged by what they found there. Its beat was newly ravenous and wild, synths and trumpets whirling in and out of focus like stage lights to inebriated eyes, Cindy Ecstasy providing an ice cool rap in which she seduces her listener to follow her down the same non-stop erotic, ecstatic New York rabbit hole she had led Almond and Ball:

If you don't believe me, ask Soft Cell, because I shook them up and I gave them hell / Call up Cindy Ecstasy if you're looking for a memory …

Chapter 8
SOHO

As much as New York shaped *Non-Stop Erotic Cabaret* and Soft Cell's second studio album, *The Art of Falling Apart*, which they began recording back at Mediasound the following summer, their music is nevertheless extremely British. More specifically, it is of Soho.

Marc Almond: *Non-Stop Erotic Cabaret* was the secret seedy life that went on behind the mask of Conservative Britain. It tells a story of a bored, ordinary bloke, seething with his life, wanting more and looking for excitement and adventure in a red neon-lit Soho world of red-light cabarets, prostitutes and sex dwarves, looking back at his youth and wondering what happened.[1]

For Almond, his path towards the West End, and Soho in particular, where flickering signs advertising illicit strip clubs and sex cinemas would reflect upwards from rainy pavements, had been laid as a teenager. At Southport Art College, a mysterious student named Fred – which was suspected to be a pseudonym – had signed up to the course late, struck up a flirtatious friendship with Almond and told tales of his time living in a neon-lit flat on Archer Street.

Marc Almond: Oh my God, I thought, not only had he lived in Soho, London, in a neon-illuminated tomb overlooking a casino, he'd also lived alongside prostitutes, junkies, pimps and creatures of the night, characters I imagined straight out of the Jean Genet novels that David Bowie had urged me to read through his songs. I made up my mind, there and then, that I too would live in Soho in such a room and with such lowlife neighbours. And so my goal was set.[2]

In 1983 Almond fulfilled that goal, renting out a flat on Brewer Street opposite the Raymond Revuebar in whose window was the neon sign reading 'Non-Stop Erotic Cabaret' from which they had taken the title of their debut album.

Tim Pope: I remember going to Marc's apartment and staring out of the window. It was like looking out at the *Non-Stop Erotic Cabaret* album cover. Marc was living the dream, living above a porn cinema or whatever it was, up some sleazy steps shared with prostitutes. I remember going out to a strip club with him and realising that the doorman flashed the person upstairs if you flashed money in your wallet. There was a pin hammer behind the bar where, if you didn't pay up, you got struck by it.

Annie Hogan: Every time I left that flat, some old man was always after me like mad. But of course it was exciting as well. Once when [Almond] was in America, he said I could stay there. Quick side story, but I took acid with Siouxsie

Sioux, then went back to Marc's and it was so strong I black-holed. He kept snakes, and I thought we were in the desert.[3]

Dave Ball: He was looking after someone's boa constrictor. The snake ended up disappearing into Soho, roaming the pavements. I never heard any police reports about it though. It's probably still in the sewers.[4]

Some Bizzare had already taken up residence in Soho, with Stevo and his increasingly esoteric roster finding office space in Trident Studios in the alleyway St Anne's Court. In the same building was the office of Rusty Egan's publishing company, and downstairs was a state-of-the-art recording studio that had been favoured by the likes of David Bowie and Queen.

Rusty Egan: It became this hub of creativity. Marc Almond had just come back from New York with Cindy Ecstasy, and I soon found out why that was her name! Every day I met more and more of these great people.

Long before Soho emerged as the nexus point for Soft Cell and Some Bizzare, Almond had already been soaking up the character of the neighbourhood and the surrounding West End. In a wilderness year between finishing his degree in 1979 and waiting for Ball to finish his own a year later, Almond was drawn there like a moth to a bulb. After collecting his giro cheque one week in Nottingham, instead of returning to the home of Huw Feather and Liz Phair with whom he was staying, he instead took a coach to London on a whim. There, he found work on the door of a Soho clip joint. His job was to sell someone a 'ticket' to a strip show or pornographic cinema around the corner, with the punter charged for a second time upon arrival at what was in fact merely an office space. Often threatened at knifepoint by those who had not taken too kindly to the con, it was not long until he returned to the relative safety of Leeds. Nevertheless, these trips continued to hold enormous influence over his work.

On one visit with Chris Neate, the two took advantage of a closing-down sale at the theatrical costumiers Charles H. Fox in Covent Garden in order to freshen up their looks for the Warehouse. As Soft Cell's early gigs in 1980 began to yield a little disposable income, he would visit more often, staying at the Chelsea home that the artist Molly Parkin had been lent by Anita Pallenberg and Keith Richards. He had become friendly with Parkin after she and her husband, Patrick Hughes, had judged his degree show, bonding too with her daughter Sophie, herself briefly an art student in Leeds.

Sophie Parkin: We had been in a minority in Leeds with the feeling that nobody's got your back, but as soon as I got to London I realised that I'd forgotten how glorious it was. You were able to go out in Soho and be as extravagant as you wanted.

Dave Ball: In New York it was full-on twenty-four-hour party people. Never mind Manchester, New York was doing it ten years earlier. But there was still good stuff in London. Heaven was always good. The gay clubs were always the best clubs because they played the best music. Whether you were gay or not it didn't really matter, you were there for the music and the vibe.[5]

Heaven had opened in December 1979 (with the Blackpool Mecca's Ian Levine as house DJ), while in 1982 Blitz organisers Rusty Egan and Steve Strange turned what had once been the Music Machine into the Camden Palace, and hosted Madonna's first British performance the following year.[6] They were the closest things London had to rival the cross-disciplinary New York mega-clubs.

Rusty Egan: I'd been to New York, all these big clubs, and I got the idea that this is clubbing: put bands on, and then it turns into a club with just DJs. In London I'd go to a pub, see a band and that was it, they'd throw you out. But I want to go out 'til three in the morning and I want to hear more music, and I've only got a fiver! So that's what led to the Camden Palace. It was LGBT friendly as well, but that community were all underground, like, 'Where's that club?' 'Well, I know a bloke …'

Annie Hogan: The Camden Palace was the first time I took ecstasy when Cindy came over, bringing her namesake with her. I had been terrified of it in Leeds, but in the Camden Palace it felt like I was in the Amazon rainforest.[7]

Rusty Egan: Every week [at The Camden Palace] I was presenting 'Here's Blancmange, here's Eurythmics, here's Yello', and every week people were saying, 'We saw this amazing band, this amazing singer, this club is fantastic', which is strange because the music industry weren't that interested. They were more interested in going to the football.

I'd go to Stevo and say, 'Got any guests for Thursday night?', and he'd have forty guests – Matt Johnson, Marc Almond, Marc Almond's friends, Marc Almond's friends' friends, Marc Almond's friends' friends' friends … Because the club was so big, we were all there, everyone was meeting everyone.

Stevo: I once got pulled aside by Steve Strange and we looked up at the balcony from the floor. He said, 'You see that tier there? People want to get there. And then to the next. And then to the final tier, which is VIP.' Kind of having a class system. I just looked at him and I didn't understand. I found it quite funny.[8]

Nevertheless, there remained something distinctly British about London's opportunities for hedonism – either advertised in euphemisms and sly winks to those in the know, or behind entirely anonymous closed doors. Because of licensing laws, after-dark clubs in Soho would have to stagger their opening hours so that when one closed another would open to accommodate drinkers who would scarper from one street to the next.

Mari Wilson, singer: Old Compton Street wasn't publicly known as a gay area, even though it was; it was much more underground. Soho then was like a secret society or a club only known to the 'in crowd' – at least that's my take on it.[9]

Tony Shrimplin, Chair, Museum of Soho: The difference between Soho in the day and at night was pronounced. As soon as the sun went down, things began to change.[10]

Soho

Soho's status as a home for the exotic, the forbidden and the thrilling goes back as far as the word itself. The name is believed to come from the hunting cry of King Henry VIII when the area was part of his grounds; the first time it appears on record is in documents related to the arrest of a sex worker, 'lewde woman' Anna Clerke, who was fined a shilling in 1641 for 'thretening to burne the houses'.[11] The settling of successive waves of immigrants – from French Huguenots fleeing anti-Protestant persecution in the sixteenth and seventeenth centuries, to Italian economic migrants in the later Victorian era – garnered it a reputation for the foreign and exotic that only intensified throughout the twentieth century.[12]

Christopher Howse, author, *Soho in the Eighties*: Soho's first golden-age flowering was in the 1950s. Before the Second World War it was unusual in its mix of foreign shops and restaurants. It had in the 1920s and 1930s the sort of night-clubs where very rich people came for fun. More people lived there than later but many were very poor. During the war it was exceptional but restricted, and the 1950s took the lid off. A second flowering was the 1980s, when young people reinforced the bohemian core. Saint Martins School of Art had its place in this. Some pubs became incredibly crowded night after night, and summer saw a swarming onto the pavements.[13]

Paul Willetts, biographer of Paul Raymond: The population of Soho varied in a way that wasn't really true of anywhere else in Britain. You'd come across Italian, French, Jewish, Maltese, Polish, Russian and Chinese people. Even by the

1970s and 1980s it still felt very distinctive, like a village within central London. A lot of its Georgian buildings were in an incredibly ramshackle state, and the shops lining those streets were shops you wouldn't really see elsewhere, which gave the whole place a frisson of the exotic. They'd be little tobacconists, delicatessens, steamy-windowed Italian cafes with espresso machines, specialist shops peddling things like ballet shoes.[14]

For those wishing to peddle pornography, prostitution and peep shows, Soho's 'continental' reputation was an easy way to market erotica; Frenchness, in particular, was a euphemism for sauciness, with its allusions to cabarets like the Folies Bergère and Moulin Rouge. In 1932, Laura Henderson, owner of the Windmill Theatre, hired a new manager called Vivian Van Damm, who, inspired directly by the French venues, managed to convince Lord Cromer, then Lord Chamberlain – whose role included deciding what needed to be censored on stage – to allow him to display nude models between variety acts, provided they stood perfectly still. Lights would dim, breasts and genitals would be slyly covered with props as the models rearranged themselves into ever more elaborate tableaus, inspired perhaps by a famous painting, a story from mythology or a historical event.[15]

Tim Arnold: My mum was a Windmill Girl, the youngest ever – she was only fifteen! Laura Henderson was passionate about having this wild place to go to in the centre of London, so they found this loophole: 'If it moves, it's rude!' It was ingenious. I think a seed was sown with the Windmill Theatre: you can be naked and not break the law. Of course, that eventually turned into an art form challenging the restrictions from our authorities to do something really daring and really human.

When Paul Raymond, the Liverpool-born entertainer who after a period as a spiv had begun his showbusiness career as a hypnotist at the end of Clacton Pier, was seeking to open the Raymond Revuebar as a permanent hub for his own touring striptease shows, he naturally gravitated towards Soho.

Paul Willetts: When he was looking for premises, Soho would have been the obvious choice because of its association with French people. The prostitutes there were known as 'Fifis' and spoke in a fake French accent. When he was touring his girlie shows around the provinces, he'd invariably title them something like Paris Nights, and a smut-seeking guy of that era would think, 'Aha! That's what I'm after'.

Tim Arnold: My grandfather Dickie Arnold was the manager for his touring show, and they had a lot of trouble in the provinces because of the nudity. My grandfather was one of the people who had to stand in the witness box and say, 'There's nothing rude', even though there definitely was.

One of the only venues in the country offering full-frontal nudity, the Revuebar was a roaring success and soon spawned imitators across Soho. Though the venue had started off with a glamorous reputation, Raymond sought further business interests that expanded into the smuttier territory of pornographic magazines. He was happy to use any scandals that arose as an opportunity for publicity, with his flamboyant fashion sense and larger-than-life persona finding him dubbed 'The King of Soho'. He also began building an enormous property portfolio. By 1977 he was buying an average of a freehold a week and was the landlord of at least one hundred buildings in the neighbourhood. By the 1990s, in an article that named him Britain's wealthiest man, he was said to own 18 per cent of Soho's eighty-seven acres, a highly conservative estimate given his use of multiple shell companies.[16]

Tim Arnold: He'd been a seaside entertainer, and a hypnotist of all things – 'Look at this hand while I'm doing that with the other.' That was a really great metaphor for what he did with Soho. He'd put on all these fantastic shows with one hand, and with the other bought up all the buildings while they were cheap.

With property prices in the West End plummeting as the 1970s financial crisis reached its peak, Raymond hoovered up buildings at auctions. While most buyers would calculate the cost of refurbishment, then base the rent on a preconceived profit margin, Raymond began by working out what amount of rent potential tenants could afford to pay.[17] Then, as soon as their lease expired, the rents would be hiked up, with shadier sex merchants more likely to be able afford the increased rent than traditional businesspeople, leading to a proliferation of further strip clubs, peep shows and brothels. The fact that rents were cheap for the first few years at least was also a boon for the itinerant artists and musicians already being drawn to Soho for its longstanding connections with culture, which had simultaneously led to a proliferation of industry headquarters, scouts and sympathetic journalists in the area. Neither they nor Raymond would likely have seen it that way, but the relationship was like that between an artist and their patron.

Tim Arnold: Fast forward to the 1960s, 1970s and 1980s, and if someone wanted to open a venue, install a jukebox somewhere, start up a management company in one of the buildings, they were free to do so and usually without a deposit. I think Paul Raymond, without even realising it, facilitated a platform.

Andrew Daniel, hairdresser at CUTS, Soho: I think he was motivated purely by money. When I first came to Soho, he got out of a big fucking motor outside our shop, a long fur coat down to the ground, with two security guards. He was hated by generations of people, but he did have a lot of properties. There were so many empty spaces, so if you had an idea, you could start a business![18]

Paul Willetts: He had a pretty terrible reputation as a landlord, but there was a lot of cheap property he was renting out.

Democratised by cheap rent, outsiders of every stripe were given room to exist, layering over one another in Soho's compact warren of alleys and doorways.

Andrew Daniel: We worked out of the basement, and to get there you had to go through a proper old-school Sicilian shop with its tiled floor and beautiful chairs. I loved that you could walk past places, but you'd never know what they really were.

Bedsit Land

You walk past and it's just two white Sicilian guys, but downstairs there's a whole other town. I remember when we first opened our shop, some guys came in and asked us for protection money. We just referred them to our landlord, Nino Polledri, and said 'Talk to him about protection money!' They apologised, 'I'm so sorry', and we never saw those guys again.

Paul Willetts: There was a quaint and reassuring side of it; lots of people knew each other and would be chatting on street corners. At the same time, though it's easy to romanticise the Soho of that era, to see it as some kind of sexual theme park, walking down alleyways at night they had a real film noir kind of menace. There was a sense that you could always make the wrong decision, ruin your life by turning down the wrong alleyway.

Andrew Daniel: There was a famous story going around about someone getting his hand chopped off with a meat cleaver by Triads over gambling debts. It was rough! That was what brought you in, as a kid you think it's quite exciting, seeing the Maltese and Chinese gangs having mass brawls, fifty strong. Going to clubs to buy weed where there was a knife on the table. But it wasn't glamorous. A lot of the women doing sex work were heroin addicts, feeding their habits. It wasn't pretty.

Soho is surrounded on all four sides by major roads. As well as walling in the district's teeming mixture of seediness and excitement, intensifying it further as it was forced to concentrate instead of spread, and providing a shield against the kind of mass development that might otherwise have been imposed on its crumbling Georgian architecture, each of those roads also brought its own footfall, from working-class and middle-class shoppers on Oxford Street to the north to the super-wealthy on Regent Street to the west. Actors, set-builders and costumiers in theatreland past Shaftesbury Avenue to the south, and bohemians drawn to second-hand bookshops and Saint Martins School of Art on Charing Cross Road to the east. Soho, the shortcut between all four, also became a melting pot for passing trade of all classes.

Tony Shrimplin: It's only three-quarters of a square mile – it warps your sense of time and space.

Until he moved there much later, Marc Almond was, in essence, just another of those passers-by, lured all the way from Leeds past Soho's artificial walls, snagged by its darkness and delights, and carrying them back with him to the north. 'Seedy Films' for instance, is in essence a walking tour of the area's back alleys. Though only one element of the personality of *Non-Stop Erotic Cabaret* – the record is just as much defined by New York's rush of drug-addled euphoria, the grittiness of post-industrial Leeds, end-of-the-pier Southport and Blackpool camp, the emotional charge of Northern Soul, Kraftwerkian electronics and the art school avant-garde – it is still Soho sleaze with which the album is most readily associated, and that Dianne Brill drew from when she plotted its bacchanalian launch party at Danceteria.

Soft Cell also drew heavily on a Soho aesthetic for their visual identity. The neon sign Huw Feather had designed for their stage shows also appears on the cover of *Non-Stop Erotic Cabaret*, along with Almond stuffing a mysterious brown paper package into his suspiciously oversized leather jacket, while Ball assumes the role of the heavy behind him, delivering a stare that demands the viewer ask no questions about what they have seen lest they find themselves in trouble. Along with Feather, long-term photographer Peter Ashworth was instrumental in establishing that aesthetic across a progression of studio shoots.

Peter Ashworth: I like the fact that I did so many shoots with Soft Cell, as it allowed us to carve out an identity. A lot of photographers back then worked for a music magazine – that was the way you got into it. You'd go to the gigs and do a few shots on the street. My gut feeling is that if they'd been working with an *NME* black and white snapper, shooting on a Nikon, they'd have been a very different band. I've never quite understood just how much the imagery around a band changes everything. It can have a massive effect. We could create these fantastic worlds to sit them in.

I was working in a basement just down the road from King's Cross; I did nearly all the Soft Cell video shoots there. It was a real little dump, but I knew that I wanted to be a studio photographer. I couldn't achieve anything special away from the studio using available light, but put me in a dark room and maybe I can start to create something I wasn't seeing anyone else doing.

One of the things that worked so well with Soft Cell is that they were really different personalities. Marc was waving, crazy, passionate; Dave was almost a machine – he wanted to do his thing, then get the hell out. And opposites in a band work so fucking well. I saw the same thing with Eurythmics later, and then again and again and again. If there's someone who's a real introvert and someone who's a real extrovert, you learn how to work it.[19]

Feather had by now assumed the role of Soft Cell's de facto art director. Thanks to his time producing ambitious plays on minimal budgets in Nottingham, he too was a master of saying a lot with mere suggestion, and was also drawing on a love of Soho's exoticism that had been present since his youth as an amateur magician.

Huw Feather: My crazy aunt lived in London all her life, where I was instantly drawn into Soho because all the famous magicians had their studios there, and when I was old enough to travel on my own at twelve, thirteen or fourteen, I would explore them all. They were like an office and a shop at the same time, a place where people would hang out. With the advent of television variety shows in the 1950s there had been a vibrant and busy time, but by the time I was cognisant, that world was in decline and they were all old men chasing after a coin. From visiting magicians' studios I got to know the vibe of the place, and I also went out to the record stores. Then I'd also see the doorways with strange postcards on the outside saying 'Models second floor please ring'. I knew about prostitution, but I didn't know that what I was looking at was prostitution. Then there'd be a doorway with a flashing neon sign that said 'X Certificate Cinema', but it was clearly leading into a basement. How could that be? There were daytime openings for the strip clubs, so there were always strange people around, but I was never, ever given any trouble. I could read the street and I knew how to stay out of it.

While Ashworth set a clear line between his work with Soft Cell in the studio and his life outside of it, Feather was spending huge swathes of his spare time in the band's company. With Ball handling most of the instrumentals, Almond took almost as much interest in visual ideas as lyrics. As a result, Soft Cell's sound and vision evolved in tandem with one another.

Huw Feather: I was living in London with Marc for three weeks out of the month, cooking, hanging out. Lyrics would get passed around and demos would get played. The ideas and visuals would start getting talked about and we would go back and forth. The artwork, the images and the visuals were there at ground level when each of the songs was composed or each of the albums was put together. The cohesion [between sound and imagery] was very structured.

Peter Ashworth: Marc was a real creator of worlds and situations, and that became something I was addicted to. *Non-Stop Erotic Cabaret* was a really reduced idea, just a few colours and a piece of plastic, PVC, and you've got Marc pretending to hide something in his jacket. The whole thing still looks vibrant.[20]

After 'Seedy Films' from *Non-Stop Erotic Cabaret* had, naturally, become a hit in Soho's strip clubs, the decision was taken to release a tie-in video album called *Non-Stop Exotic Video Show*. Tim Pope, who had previously blagged his way into helming a video for 'Bedsitter', was invited to direct a series of further promotional videos for several of the album's songs.

A wild aesthetic mixture, the videos sometimes found Soft Cell returning to their old fascination with suburbia. Pope's 'Bedsitter' video returned, while for 'Frustration' they filmed a strange psychedelic vignette, with Ball playing the dissatisfied homemaker against Almond's demonic party gnome. For 'Tainted Love', they filmed a ludicrous surrealist piece starring Almond as Emperor Caligula, tempting a small girl to put her hand in a tank of piranhas while Ball – inexplicably dressed as a cricketer, complete with batting pads – looks on.[21]

Tim Pope: I don't think that 'Tainted Love' video is the greatest piece of work to be honest, and yes, it's kind of bonkers. We only had a day to shoot each one.

At its best, however, *Non-Stop Exotic Video Show* did the same for Soho that *Non-Stop Ecstatic Dancing* had done for New York – isolating and extracting one particular influence that had gone into the original album. On 'Entertain Me', Soft Cell and Pope condense an all-night cabaret into less than four minutes of footage, a kaleidoscopic carnival of fire-breathers, snake-handlers, muscle men and jugglers. 'Seedy Films' saw Cindy Ecstasy flown over from New York for a bleary-eyed glide with the band through the West End in an open-topped car – high on ecstasy as they did so.

Tim Pope: We filmed a lot of the videos around Soho. I can't say I lived that lifestyle, but it was great fun to dip into it and to be as outrageous as we could, to cause as much trouble as possible.

The release also included 'Torch', a standalone single that came after *Non-Stop Erotic Cabaret*, which reached number two and remains the group's most successful song bar 'Tainted Love'. It features backing vocals from Cindy Ecstasy, who also appeared with them for a slinky and glamorous return to *Top of the Pops*. She was less enamoured when she found that Almond's vision for the music video involved her performing as the androgynous figure from Feather's single sleeve design, complete with bald cap.

Dave Ball: We only got held off the number-one spot because there'd been a miscount in the chart return shops. We got held off by Adam and the Ants, even though we were selling three times as many records! It's the closest we've come to one of our own songs being number one, so that's pretty irritating. But that's life![22]

Then, of course, there was 'Sex Dwarf', for which Pope hired a number of Soho sex workers and bondage practitioners to simulate orgiastic sex around Almond, while Ball played a chainsaw-wielding butcher.

Tim Pope: I got a load of meat, a load of milk, and we just had a big party! I chucked handloads of maggots in without warning anyone. Really, all that happens is a lot of posturing. People roll around in meat, a dwarf jumps out of a crate with a bondage mask on, and everyone has a load of fun. There's a fantastic end shot of Marc as he leers at the camera. I put it into slow motion and noticed that there was a writhing maggot hanging from his lip.

We filmed it in St John's Wood. We were in studio one or two, but next door some ladies of a certain age were making an aerobics video in blue leotards. I decided to break into that studio and walk through the back of their shot with the dwarf dressed in his bondage gear on the end of a lead. Somewhere there's a piece of video, these ladies dancing, with me walking through with a dwarf on a lead. It was just boys having fun!

For two former performance artists who had honed their craft among budgie murderers at Leeds Polytechnic, the 'Sex Dwarf' video was, if anything, rather tame. But after footage was leaked to the press – allegedly by the manager of the actor playing the sex dwarf – it was deemed so offensive by the tabloids that it became a national scandal, with Stevo's Some Bizzare offices being raided by the police.

Evening Standard, 15 June 1982: Stevo is unfortunately unable to provide me with a crystal-clear description of what happened. 'I spied the police from the roof,' he tells me. 'I was going to leap on their heads and pretend I was Tigger.' Thankfully, others at the studios persuaded him that this might not be a good idea and an upset was avoided.[23]

Huw Feather: It was exactly what we thought might happen. No biggie. Absolutely we were intentionally provocative because we were edgy in life. We pushed it to 100 per cent because that's what punk had delivered. Punk was a very important part of British art college at that time, and [Almond, Ball and I] were art-college trained. We had been birthed to take things to, if necessary, naughty territory. The punk value was 'fuck it'.

171

The irony, of course, is that the track had been inspired by the same tabloid sensationalism it was now on the receiving end of, after Almond saw a headline in the *News of the World* reading: 'SEX DWARF LURES 100 DISCO DOLLIES TO A LIFE OF VICE'.[24]

Dave Ball: Everyone goes on about this 'pornographic video', but when you look back on it now, it's nowhere near as bad as people think. People's imagination is much more scary than the reality – you just feed them little bits and they fill in the gaps themselves.[25]

Tim Pope: It has become a legend in its own lunchtime, mainly because it's elusive and people don't seem to have seen it. I don't even have a master copy of it.

Non-Stop Exotic Video Show is knowingly ridiculous, an act of silliness above all else. The videos were tied together by scrappy, ad-libbed segments from Almond and Ball – the former giddy and giggly like an inebriated children's TV presenter, the latter awkward and almost silent. To introduce 'Tainted Love', a gruff, Pythonesque cleaning lady skewers the song's enduring status as Soft Cell's mainstream hit – 'You know, when I see 'em on *Top of the Pops* I think, "Oh my god, what are they?" But I love this one, I think it's great. Rest of it's rubbish though. Absolute rubbish.'[26]

Elsewhere Almond reads directly from tabloid reports about the song and revels melodramatically in the hysteria, and later dips into a Soho porn cinema where a furtive cashier informs him the 'Sex Dwarf' video is now showing. 'Not the super-shocking, scandalous, dwarf-exploiting, meat-cleaving, girl-whipping Soft Cell video I've read so much about?!' gasps Almond expectantly, direct to camera. 'Er, no, the other version,' says the cashier. Phonogram had only let the band include a censored 'Sex Dwarf' on the eventual *Non-Stop Exotic Video Show*, with Almond and the sex workers from the video dressed as choristers.

Tim Pope: I don't think the record company loved it. Here was this band who had had massive success with 'Tainted Love', 'Bedsitter' had gone to number four, but then we made 'Sex Dwarf'! Basically, I don't think they had been ready for the massive success that 'Tainted Love' had. They were kind of an arts band that were dicking around and having fun, then suddenly found this huge success. Within a year we were undermining that success in a pretty epic way! We knew we were causing trouble; I don't think I became the favourite person for the record company after that, but Soft Cell were co-conspirators.

At a show at a night club called Cinderella's in provincial Sussex, they experimented with showing the original 'Sex Dwarf' video live. Dropping acid before their arrival in a chauffeur-driven limo, Almond, Ball, Feather and their friend Jane Rolink, soon to get a job at Some Bizzare, arrived to find Stevo Djing a mixture of Throbbing Gristle and a novelty record featuring the children's TV characters Sooty and Sweep – the latter of whom communicated only through high pitched honks – covering the music hall standard 'The Laughing Policeman'. When projectors began playing the 'Sex Dwarf' video, things boiled over among an already unimpressed crowd into a full-blown riot. Barricading themselves in their dressing room, when they eventually escaped, the group found their limo smashed to pieces.

Tim Pope: I think the original 'Sex Dwarf' was only ever shown once. I remember Marc phoning us up – he'd taken some hallucinogenic drug or another and had to escape from a riot through a bathroom window.

Marc Almond, interviewed by *NOISE!* magazine, 8 July 1982: We decided to try the video out on people, which was an impulsive thing that could have been right or wrong, but the club says we started the trouble by showing it. […] It was the most frightening experience I've had in my whole life, with people threatening to break my legs. It was a nightmare, and now everyone's saying I should get security. After it was all over, I just sat in the bathroom and cried for two hours. It was such a shock, it was too much. Why should I have to put up with it? I should be enjoying myself. I was saying to someone the other day that I used to be really extrovert, but now I find I'm becoming the opposite. When I go out, I just want to sit in corners and I'm a bag of nerves all time, I feel nervous talking to people.[27]

'Proper' live performances, unencumbered by mobs, were few and far between. When they did appear, the band still favoured the chaotic little club shows on which they had made their name, rather than stepping up to venues befitting their new-found status.

Dave Ball: We were nervous of them. Depeche Mode always went on big tours as soon as they could, but for us the idea of doing night after night, we just didn't want to do it, so we didn't! We were offered to be the support act for David Bowie, but we turned it down.[28]

Marc Almond: I don't remember the tour offer with David Bowie, but Dave assures me we were offered that and that we said no because we just didn't think we were good enough to be on the bill with him. I'm glad in a way because Bowie remained a distant hero all my life and though I had the chance, I never met him. He never let me down. We were bruised by constant jibes and criticism and, in our hearts, still felt like the poor northerners. We didn't want to be seen in a bad light with Bowie. 'They're all gonna laugh at you!' So it figures.[29]

The show at Cinderella's had been both a violent flashpoint and indicative of the wider way in which Soft Cell were received by the public when they strayed from their more palatable pop hits. Rowan Atkinson, on the popular satirical show *Not the Nine O'Clock News*, summed up much of this viewpoint in his impression of Almond, portraying him as a weedy, affected, pretentious and preening one-hit wonder.[30] Almond's private life became the stuff of (primarily false) tabloid speculation.

Evening Standard, 7 June 1982: THIS attractive couple are Soft Cell's Marc Almond and New Yorker Cindy Ecstasy [...] They met last year at Studio 54 and Cindy spent last Christmas at Marc's house getting over a broken love-affair. In February, much to my surprise, the relationship blossomed into a romance [...] and a lovey-dovey weekend at Florida's Disneyworld.[31]

At the same time, a gruelling promotional schedule at the behest of Phonogram was only adding more grist to that mill, placing further strains on their working relationship.

Mike Thorne: I think 'Torch' was recorded when Marc and Dave were barely speaking to each other. They were really on edge; it was a bit 'please ask your mother to pass the salt'. Ironically, 'Torch' is one of the best things we did together. I think the record company, in their wisdom, had flown them in from a promotional tour of Turkey or something, direct to New York. 'Tainted Love' was such an enormous hit worldwide that the record company wanted them everywhere.[32]

Tensions between Almond and Ball never quite boiled over into a full-blown row – Phonogram provided enough of a common enemy to keep them broadly united – but when they returned to New York to record their next album, *The Art of Falling Apart*, the distance between them was notable. The giddiness that had defined their earlier sessions had long since dissipated. Where before the band and their friends had lived together in the Mediasound apartment, now Ball was spending most of his spare time – to Almond's jealousy – with Anita Sarko at her Greenwich Village apartment.

Harvey Goldberg: They were already getting burnt out. I believe Dave and Marc were still getting along, but they were starting to move in very different circles. Nothing acrimonious, they were just drifting apart as people.

Dave Ball: We'd had a taste of being the pop band; we'd done every stupid radio and TV show around Europe, doing endless 'Tainted Love' interviews, sometimes twenty a day and with all the same questions. If this was what it was like being a pop band, we didn't want to continue and make another record that was as obvious as the first one.[33]

Marc Almond: We fought against the pigeonhole that Phonogram were trying to push us into and a twee pop image. It was fun for a while and we both weren't anti-pop, we were both pop music fans. We just felt we were being pushed into a dishonest corner. The nadir [was] being on the cover of *Smash Hits* in party hats, like two clowns. We had to kill that dead … We rebelled and decided to go in a different direction. Soft Cell as an electro rock duo.[34]

Beverley Glick: I remember doing an interview with Marc in New York, and he just couldn't cope with it all. He just found it really, really hard, emotionally and psychologically, to deal with the way that he was being treated, and not just by the media. He had so many obsessive fans – he had an entire family stalking him at one point. He had gone from being this this skinny boy from Leeds doing fairly left-field things to this mainstream figure appearing on American chat shows, and he just found that really, really hard to cope with. And that, obviously, led to insane drug-taking and musically going down a very dark path. He hated what the media tried to make him become; he got very angry about that.

The band's drugs of choice had moved from the heady joys of early ecstasy into darker climes defined by heavy psychedelics like LSD and mescaline mixed in among cocaine – a decision to include a medley of Jimi Hendrix songs was taken after they dropped tabs of acid called Purple Haze just as the song of the same name coincidentally started playing on a nearby stereo. Symbolically, Cindy Ecstasy herself was gradually moving away from the Soft Cell camp following their argument over her going bald for the 'Torch' video, and the failure of a planned sham marriage through which both she and Almond were to claim dual British-American citizenship. She formed a short-lived band of her own with Rick Holliday called Six Sed Red, before disappearing from public view entirely.

Marc Almond: I don't know what became of her after that. Someone told me that she had a guest house in some seaside town in Britain somewhere, that she's running a hotel. But I have no idea![35]

When all of this combined with their long-held desire to move as far away as possible from the straight-up pop of 'Tainted Love' that had become such a millstone around their neck, and Almond's need for a creative outlet for the anger he felt over his treatment in the media, it made for an altogether darker and more expansive record. Taken just nine months after his sleeve for *Non-Stop Erotic Cabaret* – playful in its sleaziness, a sly wink to the camera – Peter Ashworth's cover for *The Art of Falling Apart* is stark and nightmarish, Almond and Ball's faces partly covered by cracked masks, washed up on a shore littered with memorabilia, remnants from a pop career now dead.

Peter Ashworth: Huw turned up with a bag of tricks, bits of jewellery, this, that and the other. These trinkets that were significant to Marc and Dave. We laid enough sand on the ground to cover half their bodies and that was it. It was Stevo's idea to shoot under different colour gels, a golden one and a pinky, dirtied-up one, which gave it a claustrophobic atmosphere.[36]

The masks used on the front cover were those Almond had used during some of his university performances, indicative of the way much of the record saw them returning to their darker art roots. Lyrics, for instance, returned to the kinds of artistic, esoteric and underground influences they had soaked up at Leeds. 'Numbers', a bleak and nihilistic account of the emptiness felt after anonymous hook-ups was named after a novel by the writer John Rechy, documenting gay subculture in the 1960s, while 'Kitchen Sink Drama' was an ode to the domestic 1950s melodramas of director Douglas Sirk. The themes of lust and desire common in many of Tennessee Williams's plays held great influence across the record, with the dizzy 'Baby Doll' named in tribute to both Elia Kazan's film of the same name, an adaptation of Williams's subversive one-act play *27 Wagons Full of Cotton*, and the Baby Doll Lounge in New York where they had observed lonely men stuffing money into the underwear of scantily clad bar dancers. 'Martin', which had been extant in demo form since the Leeds days, recounts the plot of George A. Romero's 1977 horror about a troubled boy who murders and drinks blood from his victims in the belief he is a vampire.[37]

The band's recording home of New York, too, was turning darker as rents began to rise, clubbers dabbled with heroin and AIDS ravaged the city with ever-increasing intensity, which had a particular impact on the gay culture that underpinned so much of its cultural vitality. The Mineshaft was among the first clubs to be closed by the New York City Department of Health in 1985, who contended that it permitted 'high-risk sexual activity'.[38]

Jack Fritscher: The titanic 1970s had been a first-class party to cruise on, ignorant of the iceberg of HIV that lay ahead. Nearly everybody died, some survived. AIDS drove a stake through the heart of nightlife. But, and this is extremely important, clubs like the Mineshaft did not cause AIDS. In fact, it was [in] the clubs where people shot up with needles that AIDS got transferred more. The needle did more damage than sex at the clubs.

Richard Boch: Pre-AIDS, everyone was free, willing to fuck at the end of the night and willing to go home with anyone, male or female. There were less lines in the sand at that time.

Josephine Warden: AIDS just completely smashed everything. That's when it finished, our little fabulous moment in time.[39]

Marc Almond: It became more and more visible. Places closed down and the whole landscape of New York seemed to change. It seemed to go very dark, desperate, fearful and unfriendly.[40]

Pamina Brassey: It was in 1983 that the *Time* magazine article about AIDS came out, and it felt like everything changed. We all felt that we were going to die. People were spreading rumours, that it was a Republican solution to kill gay people. It was really scary.

Although neither was written about the AIDS epidemic, both 'Numbers' and 'Martin' – the latter with its mentions of blood-drinking and 'an illness flowing through him' – became imbued with bleak new subtext. The same would happen to 'Tainted Love', when in 1985 the experimental duo Coil reinterpreted the title to refer to the disease and released an intense, funereal cover version, singer Jhonn Balance recording with his arm restrained behind his back in order to imbue the vocals with more pain, along with a harrowing video depicting the death of an AIDS patient (featuring a cameo from Almond as a leather-clad angel of death).[41] With proceeds going to the Terrence Higgins Trust, it was the first musical release to serve as an AIDS benefit.

Ball, meanwhile, was trying to assert himself as a producer capable of more than the oft-parodied 'dink-dink' of 'Tainted Love'. Having spent much of his free time after the debut album hoarding new experimental demos, he brought thicker and more complex layers of sound via an upgrade of equipment – the beefy tones of the Oberheim DMX/Linn drum machine and the polyphonic Prophet 5 synth in place of the relatively tinny Roland 808 on which he had written 'Tainted Love' – and a new-found fascination with sampling bass guitar to be mixed with synth bass, in the style of the great funk producers.[42] As with Almond's lyrics, film soundtracks like *The Shining* and *Psycho* – the latter of which the pair watched together on an acid trip – were influential.

Dave Ball, speaking to *Melody Maker*, 15 January 1983: For me, the first album was a terrifying situation, because we had this collection of songs and this massive record company putting pressure on us – they know you're naive, they know your weaknesses – and so we thought 'Well, we've gotta have pop tunes because they want singles.' I'm not saying I disown any of that material because I don't – some of it's good – but I can allow myself a bit more leeway now, and I've tended to experiment a bit more. At that time we were just glad to be getting the records out whereas now I think we're really using the business to put something across. That's always been the intention, right from the start – it's just that somebody suddenly managed to channel it commercially. Really, I don't care if we never get another record in the charts, I'm not really bothered.[43]

Mike Thorne: They were trying to assert themselves. Whether they had the skills was another matter. They got very pushy, and I thought, 'I'm not going to argue every single point'. I did the right things, pushed the right buttons, and the record came out at the end of it. It's still not a bad record. I found myself caught in the middle. The band thinks I'm answering to the record company, and the record company thinks I'm getting in with the band.[44]

Colin Bell: The process of making a record involves a relationship between the musicians and the A&R people.

Marc had a lot of tastes and a lot of views and an outlook as an artist, and there would have been a clash between the kinds of records that the record company felt they could sell, which were dance pop records, and some of the stuff that Marc wanted to sing. There's always a creative tension between the record company and the artists, and very often, to be honest with you, the record company are right. The very best record executives are not insensitive to artists at all.

Dave Ball: 'Numbers' probably wasn't the wisest track to release as a single, considering it was the beginning of the AIDS epidemic. It wasn't ideal marketing for this chart band to release a song talking about anonymous sex. The album didn't produce any hit singles. We were stupid; if we'd put 'Torch' on *The Art of Falling Apart*, it probably would have done a lot better – a sticker on the front advertising the track that was number two in the charts probably would have made all the difference.[45]

Although, at Phonogram's insistence, both the Hendrix medley and 'Martin' were cut from the initial edition of the album's vinyl release, included instead on a twelve-inch vinyl packaged along with early pressings or as bonus tracks on the CD edition, the increased heft that Soft Cell swung behind *The Art of Falling Apart* was rewarded with reviews far more favourable than *Non-Stop Erotic Cabaret* ever received.

Record Mirror, 8 January 1983: David's ideas and playing and the power of Marc's voice refuse to leave you untouched. Soft Cell take risks. Look at things most people try to ignore.

Speak of the unspoken. That's why they're still one of the most interesting groups making music for today.[46]

Melody Maker, 23 January 1983: The trouble with Almond and Ball is they can't let a good idea or go and usually push on in search of an excuse to use it. That's why there's the occasional blinder of a line set amidst some rather dull dialogue. But so what, there are more than enough high spots to make it worth the journey.[47]

Dave Ball: *Non-Stop Erotic Cabaret* was our pop album, whereas *The Art of Falling Apart* was much more grown up. It was more true to our original idea of Soft Cell, a lot darker and heavier. Too heavy for some people – we lost a lot of the pop fans.[48]

Acclaim for this darker artistic vision did not translate into the kind of sales Phonogram were hoping for. In an effort to rectify this, behind Almond, Ball and Stevo's backs, the distributor packaged the single release of 'Numbers' with the B-side 'Barriers' along with a copy of 'Tainted Love' as a sweetener for the consumer. Arriving at Phonogram's headquarters, Almond smashed gold discs on the wall, while Stevo uprooted a pot plant and set off a fire extinguisher in the business affairs department.

Marc Almond speaking to *Melody Maker*, 12 March 1983: It's a small thing but, as people, we should have the right to do that and when somebody comes along and cheapens it behind our backs in a very sneaky sort of way, it's not only kicking us in the face, it's kicking Soft Cell fans in the face as well. It's not the company that suffers for that, it's the band because people turn round and say 'That's a bit of a cheap sort of thing to do isn't it?' and I quite agree, I feel ashamed. I mean, not only did they not want 'Numbers' out in the first place, they don't want anything we do to come out, they want something else.[49]

Dave Ball: I wasn't in London at the time, but next thing I heard was that Marc and Stevo had gone to New Bond Street where the headquarters of Phonogram was, got in there and started smashing. I think it was mostly Status Quo's gold discs, because their name also began with S. I think Stevo threw a cup of coffee over the MD, which isn't really the best working relationship. Never mind the Sex Pistols, here's Soft Cell![50]

The planned third single from *The Art of Falling Apart*, 'Loving You, Hating Me', was never released.

Chapter 9

WE COULD GO OUT TO DINNER
BUT WE'RE ALWAYS ON DRUGS

In 1983, several of the world's most radical avant-garde musicians had all ended up living on Beck Road, an otherwise unassuming terraced street in Hackney, London, thanks in part to the charity Acme, which offered affordable housing for artists. At number four was David Tibet, whose fascination with the occultist Aleister Crowley, mysticism and religion had driven him to form the project Current 93 the previous year. Tibet had also briefly been a member of Psychic TV, whose leader Genesis P-Orridge lived at number fifty. At numbers forty-eight and fifty-two, P-Orridge had arranged legalised squats, where Alex Fergusson (another soon-to-be-member of Psychic TV), members of the industrial band 23 Skidoo and also Tibet would all at some point find themselves living.[1] Members of Thee Temple ov Psychick Youth, co-founded by P-Orridge as a sprawling collective dedicated to transgressive art and chaos magick, were to be spotted marching in the street.

At number eleven was Patrick Moore (later known as the writer Philip Hoare to avoid association with the astronomer of the same name), who was running the record label

We could go out to dinner but we're always on drugs

Operation Twilight, the UK branch of Belgian DIY imprint Les Disques du Crépuscule.

Philip Hoare: It was a romantically Dickensian piece of decay, that whole area. The canal was full of shopping trolleys and buggies. I remember the doctors was underneath an early Victorian terraced house, it was like *The Elephant Man*. And you were very close to the City of London, living this incredibly debauched life. The new Broadgate buildings were rising up in the phallic city. The 55 bus journey up the Hackney Road felt like a transitional thing as you left behind that residual dark heart. Even though Hackney was a dangerous place, I felt safe there. It was uncommodified and there was no one making money off us.[2]

At number twelve was JG Thirlwell of Scraping Foetus off the Wheel, whose music was abrasive in the extreme. For many of them, their gathering place of choice was the offices of Some Bizzare.

JG Thirlwell: It was our hangout because it was so central. When you first got involved with the label, it was where you'd go to see what was going on, where people were going that night.[3]

Rather than use the surprise success of 'Tainted Love', and the reputational boost given by the success of *Some Bizzare Album* alumni Depeche Mode, Blancmange and The The – the last of whom remained on his roster – as an opportunity to make further strides into the mainstream, Stevo used popular success as leverage with which to continue in the mission he had first embarked upon with his DJ sets and his futurist chart: to bring challenging, disruptive, boundary-pushing music to as many ears as possible. Psychic TV had been among the label's first signings for their album *Force the Hand of Chance*, and within a year they had released *Dreams Less Sweet* via CBS, with the MD's office chair being handed over to Some Bizzare. Cabaret Voltaire and Einstürzende Neubauten would soon follow. Stevo's offices in Soho had emerged as the nexus point for the most exciting music on earth.

Stevo: 1983 was a great year for Some Bizzare. The office would have been extremely busy; we had a lot of productions going on at that time.[4]

Peter Ashworth: I was there one day when Genesis P-Orridge and [Throbbing Gristle and Psychic TV bandmate] Peter Christopherson were carrying this skull around, a real human skull which I'm not sure they could legally own, and talking about 3D homophonic recording – something to do with putting microphones inside people's heads. They were playing me these tapes I had to listen to with headphones on, a recording of a matchbox being shaken around your head, and you had to work out what number it was shaking out. That sort of thing was happening at Some Bizzare all the time.[5]

Martin McCarrick, Soft Cell touring musician, Mambas member: Thee Temple ov Psychick Youth would meet there. They had a very striking look about them – shaved heads with a ponytail at the back, piercings and tattoos that in 1983 were still quite unusual. That piercing and body manipulation scene wasn't really happening in the UK back then.[6]

Phillip Hoare: Thee Temple ov Psychick Youth used to march up Beck Road with a candlelight procession to hold a vigil outside St Joseph's Hospice at the end of the road, which in retrospect was so deeply insensitive as to be unbelievable!

The Some Bizzare offices were chaotic, but it was a chaos amid which a sense of unfettered productivity was still able to thrive.

Annie Hogan: It was mental there – great, but mental, especially if you weren't prepared for it. Leeds had been pretty wild in its own way, but it was nothing like going down to experience the crazy Stevo and his circus. It was an amazing place of conflict but unbelievable creativity. You might hear shouting or things being thrown.[7]

Martin McCarrick: Jane Rolink was great, a very down-to-earth Barnsley girl who said it how it was. She had a good relationship with Stevo because she wouldn't let him get away with things as much.

Annie Hogan: There would always be a load of fans hanging around outside too, squeezed into black outfits.[8]

JG Thirlwell: It was this gaggle of Marc maniacs, all dressed as Marc Almond clones. They seemed to always be there; I don't know if they turned up at ten and stayed 'til six? I don't know why they weren't in school. I would turn up, and then after a while they started to know who I was and they'd go, 'Oh, is Marc coming? Is Marc up there?' He would stop and talk to them and sign autographs. He had to walk through that every day. He was also living just around the corner too.

Later dubbed the Gutterhearts by Lydia Lunch of the parallel New York outsider music scene – who had struck up a friendship with Almond and a number of the Some Bizzare collective – the crowds outside the office were a stark reminder that Soft Cell were in many ways the outliers at Some Bizzare, the gargantuan pop darlings of 'Tainted Love', 'Torch' and 'Say Hello, Wave Goodbye' in the darkness of whose shadow these avant-garde noise pushers were being given room to flourish. Yet despite their stardom, Soft Cell were far from pariahs among Some Bizzare's increasingly esoteric community, nor were they tourists flitting in and out to pick up a bit of darkness for their sound; they were every ounce as integral.

JG Thirlwell: Where they came from was still art school, performance art and stuff like that. 'Memorabilia' was a fast and stormy electronic thing that didn't really have much to do with 'Tainted Love'. It just so happened that 'Tainted Love' really caught on with people, and so they got co-opted, covered by all the pop magazines. On one hand, Marc was happy to ride that wave; on the other, he was still very interested in counterculture, experimental and darker music, whether that was Scott Walker, Jacques Brel or what Psychic TV were doing.

Billy McGee, Soft Cell touring musician, Mambas member: Soft Cell were dark, sometimes malevolent![9]

We could go out to dinner but we're always on drugs

Annie Hogan: To me they were always experimental. Dave remixing 'Downtown' in our shared house in Leeds through a synth – that was not pop. They were mixing a pop sensibility with experimental avant-garde.[10]

The Some Bizzare crowd would also gather at Stevo's house in Hammersmith – where Almond also lived for a time.

JG Thirlwell: I guess it was the house that 'Tainted Love' built. Jane Rolink was living there, and Zeke Manyika. That's where I got to know Marc; we got along really well. At one point, Stevo took an axe to the bathroom door, so if you closed it there was a big hole in it. I don't know if that was his way of telling us to leave or not.

For more intimate nights out, better suited to their opaque aesthetics, they gravitated around the Batcave, first held in Soho's Gargoyle Club and then a succession of nearby venues, playing a part in what would be looked back on as a formative moment in the development of goth.

JG Thirlwell: The Batcave is thought of as the ground zero for goth now, but at the time I don't know if we were using that word. It wasn't the way we think of goth now, an identikit thing of white face makeup, black clothes and spiky hair.

Martin McCarrick: The Palace had lasers. You'd see people like Boy George, Marilyn and Fun Boy Three as well as Nick Cave; it was a melting pot of music and art. But the Batcave was more exotic. It was very, very dark. Very sleazy. It felt like you were going down into the depths of hell. There were lots of white faces, like a Wes Craven horror type of scene. There were a lot of androgynous-looking people – women with shaved heads, men with makeup. There were lots of black clothes, lots of leather and studs. It was almost a like the music scene and the fetish scene had collided.

Annie Hogan: Everybody from Some Bizzare used to go, Nick Cave was there, Lydia Lunch often came down, Siouxsie Sioux, Kid Congo Powers when he was over with the Gun Club. It was all the cool outsiders and freaks. They asked me to do a guest DJ set on the stairs, next to Danielle Dax in her cage, naked and painted as a bird of paradise or something. I was encouraged to just play whatever I wanted, John Barry and big band to electronic music. It was fantastic if you could get in.[11]

It was one night in the Batcave that Anne Stephenson and Gini Hewes (later Gini Ball after her marriage to Dave) met Marc Almond. The two were classically trained violinists who had been through the Guildhall School of Music and Drama, but also punk fans who funded their studies through busking as part of a trio called Humoresque with cellist Caroline Lavelle, who was studying at the Royal College of Music. Shows might include Stephenson playing 'Flight of The Bumblebee' while dressed as a bee, or Lavelle performing flying splits while the others played a manic version of Vivaldi's 'Four Seasons'.[12]

Anne Stephenson: We were punks, which of course was really frowned upon at Guildhall. I was always being told off. Most classical players wouldn't be seen dead being a punk.

We could go out to dinner but we're always on drugs

We ended up playing with Siouxsie and the Banshees on their *A Kiss in the Dreamhouse* tour. I think it was in the *News of the World* that we saw this big central spread about Soft Cell. Gini and I had been listening on repeat to *Non-Stop Erotic Cabaret* in our flat in Peckham, and I said, 'Look at this amazing article on Soft Cell. Wouldn't it be great if we could play with them?'[13]

Gini Ball: Later, we went to the Batcave and unbelievably Marc was standing at the bar. I said to Anne, 'Go ask him if he ever wants strings!'[14]

Anne Stephenson: I'm the chatterbox one, I said 'Marc, we're classically trained violin players', even though we were completely goth and punk looking. 'We want to play with you! We love you!' He said, 'That'd be fantastic! Come into the Some Bizzare offices tomorrow and we'll work it out.' We couldn't believe it!

Gini Ball: He'd just started a new album with the Mambas. It wasn't long after that we were in the studio.

An amorphous band, the Mambas had already been active as early as the immediate aftermath of *Non-Stop Erotic Cabaret* in one form or another, broadly serving as a vehicle for Almond to dip back into the darkness in which Soft Cell had formed and pursue eclectic personal fascinations, from flamenco music to French chanson. His old friend from Leeds, Annie Hogan, was the only collaborator who spanned its entire existence.

Annie Hogan: After Soft Cell had had their hit and every-thing, Marc bought a house in Headingley and I moved into a room in the loft. He also got me a poodle and insisted on calling him Pervert. I was chasing him round the park shout-ing 'Pervy! Pervy!' I brought my piano and moved that into the basement, and that was where I wrote [the Mambas track] 'Black Heart'.[15]

After Hogan rediscovered her considerable talent for the piano, in which she had been trained prior to coming to Leeds and making a diversion into Djing, The The's Matt Johnson introduced her to the composer Simon Fisher Turner, with whom she started collaborating.

Anni Hogan: I had done this piano solo on this cassette and I played it to Marc. I remember him being like, 'Wow', because it is pretty great, and saying 'Oh, you play piano?' I don't think I'd been keeping it a secret – I just don't think I'd told him. The first track we did was 'Fun City', which ended up being the B-side to 'Say Hello, Wave Goodbye'.[16]

Described as being recorded 'for Marc and the Mambas', the track appeared once again in a muddier form on the first standalone Mambas release, backed with a sprawling experimental electro jam called 'Sleaze (Take It and Shake It)', released only to Soft Cell's fan club. An acid-fuelled debut album compiled from covers of Scott Walker, Lou Reed, Jacques Brel and Syd Barrett – as well as a smatter-ing of originals – called *Untitled* followed on Phonogram in September. With Matt Johnson of The The joining as a cen-tral member, to record they made use of the state-of-the-art studio in the basement of Trident House and worked through the night. Phonogram, by this point, were not to bother intervening.

Colin Bell: By this stage [Almond and Ball] would have made money. For the first few years you're in debt to the record company; they want a fair amount of control because they want to get their money back. Once you get past that point you can pretty much make the record you want to and ask the record company to sell it for you. You should by then be experienced enough to know the pitfalls and be able to do it yourself, so the nature and the balance of the relationship changes. For some artists that works, and for others it doesn't.

JG Thirlwell: Marc was very restless and very prolific. I would say that the Mambas was his way to funnel those different musical interests in a place where he, as an artist, could have a bit more gravity than people perceived in Soft Cell, who were probably being pressurised to be a hit machine.

Annie Hogan: We recorded late at night, on cheap time. You'd find us there [at Trident House] at three in the morning, along with Flood engineering. We met John Barry as he was overrunning on a James Bond theme – he was my hero – and I shook his hand. His wife then just spent the whole night slagging off John Williams.

I think *Untitled* was a great release for Marc. That he felt he could be himself a lot more. He was himself in Soft Cell, but with the Mambas it wasn't also disguised as pop. It was a different thing altogether. We were listening to Scott

Walker a lot, a load of 1960s stuff, the Velvet Underground, and sharing a lot of interests. To me it was the musical arrangements of Angela Morley, these mind-blowing orchestral arrangements that enabled Scott Walker to deliver these fantastic vocals, these gorgeous tones that came along with a dramatic performance. I was very much influenced by the idea of what we could do with Marc. He couldn't keep time in the same way; he had his own timing, but that worked brilliantly.[17]

Anne Stephenson: The night we met Marc, he said, 'We've got a concert next week at Drury Lane – you can play with us.' I don't remember rehearsing. We said, 'Oh, can we have some pedals to add distortion and stuff?' At that point we were trying to be experimental. So they sent a runner to go buy these pedals, even though we hadn't even heard the songs. We just improvised; it was kind of mad. We also supported with Humoresque and did our set, fast and furious kind of stuff.

Annie Hogan: It was my first ever gig. I had to walk on and play the grand piano by myself to begin with and I was a nervous wreck. I had some sheet music that I immediately knocked on the ground. It was still a fantastic show, and then Soft Cell came on for the encore and there was just screaming, which felt a bit odd. Then we did a gig in the Batcave, just me and Marc with strings, and it felt like we were the Velvet Underground. We supported Siouxsie and the Banshees a few times, which was more challenging. Their audiences hated us, but we went on and defied them.[18]

We could go out to dinner but we're always on drugs

Though the Mambas' debut received barely any promotion from Phonogram, the group continued as an ongoing project operating in parallel with Soft Cell, constantly expanding to include more and more of the musicians orbiting Some Bizzare as they embarked on a follow-up, *Torment and Toreros*. Steve Sherlock, who had joined The The after his time in *Some Bizzare Album*-featured Neu Electrikk, became a pivotal member, while JG Thirlwell of Foetus made occasional appearances under his Frank Want alias. Others were poached from more reputable environs, such as Stephenson and Gini Ball. After their Humoresque bandmate Caroline Lavelle departed to join Terry Hall's post-Specials project Fun Boy Three, the remaining violinists then lured in fellow Guildhall students Billy McGee and Martin McCarrick as her replacement.

Anne Stephenson: Caroline was getting a bit upset. She was the one who used to drive us around in her car, paying for petrol, and she said, 'I'm not a charity. I can't keep playing for no money.' I didn't blame her. We could barely afford to eat at the time. But I thought, 'Well, Fun Boy Three are alright, but they're not as good as Marc!' I recognised Marc as a genius. At the time I would have starved to play with him; it was so thrilling to work with him, watching him come up with brilliant lyrics and melodies, writing a whole song in a matter of minutes.

Martin McCarrick: Me and Billy McGee, who I was flat-sharing with at the time, would busk, so we'd bump into each other on that scene too. Anne Stephenson called me up one day, she'd been working with Marc, and said, 'We're trying to get more strings together'.

Billy McGee: Trident was the studio where Bowie had recorded *Hunky Dory*. I was absolutely starstruck. The album was recorded in two ten-day sessions from ten o'clock at night to six o'clock in the morning. It was an incredible thing for me, but I had to keep working in college, and they didn't like it at all that I was doing 'pop music', which is what they termed it.

JG Thirlwell: Matt was already off, probably doing [The The album] *Soul Mining*, so it changed and became a nucleus around Annie Hogan. She was kind of like the musical director, coming up with a lot of stuff. Marc was incredible at listening to that music, sitting in the studio and scribbling out lyrics and coming up with vocal melodies on the spot.

Gini Ball: There was a lot of improvising. Marc would give us little ideas of what he wanted, sing us something, then leave it to us to work out the arrangement.

It saw psyches pushed to their limits, especially for those, like the Guildhall students, who were still attempting to maintain their 'ordinary' lives in parallel.

Martin McCarrick: We'd work through the night, and then even if we finished at three o'clock in the morning, we'd often end up going to the Batcave or somewhere else for a drink afterwards. I'd get home at about five, then get up at eight to go to orchestra rehearsal, pretending I was all fresh.

Billy McGee: Everybody else went home when we finished, but for me and Martin we'd have a shower then go into college. He was in a chamber orchestra and I was in a symphony orchestra. We had lessons and exams. I had such bad sleep deprivation that my partner said I was screaming in my sleep that God was talking to me. I was in a terrible state. I think you can hear that on the album!

Annie Hogan: The Mambas was very speedy because you could get a wrap super cheap. Speed and weed. You can see it in everybody's eyes in the photographs. Steve Sherlock got hold of these Black Bombers. Emotions were on the edge. Out of that came great music, but, you know, we were getting no sleep. We were tired, wasted, then flying, then exhausted again.[19]

Billy McGee: We weren't staying up on coffee, you know?

Anne Stephenson: I didn't take coke or anything like that. I've always been able to stay up late when I get excited. It's my interest in things that keeps me going.

Boundaries between the Mambas and Soft Cell often blurred. Thirlwell, for instance, became a regular at Soft Cell shows and television performances, where he would bark like a rabid hound through a manic cover of Suicide's 'Ghost Rider'. Though they were not singers, the string section of Gini Ball, Stephenson, McGee and McCarrick – now dubbed the Venomettes by Some Bizzare's Jane Rolink – were repurposed as backing vocalists the same day they signed up for the Mambas.

Gini Ball: He wanted some backing vocalists, so why not ask the string players?

Martin McCarrick: Although we could carry a tune, we definitely weren't singers, but we were broke, so we said 'Of course!' It was that afternoon we ended up in a rehearsal with Soft Cell. There was no audition, we just went in, stood behind some microphones and went from there.

Along with saxophonist Gary Barnacle, the Venomettes then embarked on tour with Soft Cell to promote *The Art of Falling Apart*, moving forward in sporadic chunks of shows. A triumphant set at the Hammersmith Palais in March was followed by dates across Europe that month.

Billy McGee: It was a sliding doors moment. My life up until that point was going to be: work my way up through the provincial orchestras, hopefully get into a London orchestra, then the symphony orchestra. Next thing I know, I'm on tour with this mental synth band. I had to get permission from college to go!

Annie Hogan: I Djed on that tour; I have good memories of it. Huw did this very camp, theatrical set with flames coming out of it when they played 'Heat'. I could play whatever I wanted; it was exciting. There were a hell of a lot of drugs around so it was quite draining, but you don't think of like that at the time. You're doing art![20]

We could go out to dinner but we're always on drugs

Gini Ball: Foetus came on stage for 'Ghost Rider' and it went really mad. Marc was this rock star – the microphone stand was thrown to the floor.

Martin McCarrick: I remember swearing to myself that I'd never do a show like that again. It was just insane. People were fainting, being carried off across the stage. Having done lots of classical concerts, it felt like Beatlemania. It was a bit horrific seeing people being crushed, thinking 'Is this actually safe?'

In April, the Mambas then picked up the baton for three severely under-rehearsed shows at the Duke of York's Theatre.

Peter Ashworth: I had done a bit of timpani drums for them, and Marc asked if I could come on stage to do it. I said, 'Sure', but no one said, 'But just for that one track'. I don't think there was any kind of rehearsal, and nobody explained what I was actually meant to do, so at the end of the track I'm still standing there. Marc is giving me these looks like, 'What the fuck are you still doing on stage? Fuck off!' My credit on *Torment and Toreros* is Peter (Once On Stage You'll Never Get Him Off) Ashworth.[21]

Billy McGee: It was an absolute fiasco. We didn't have any rehearsal, so when we went on stage it was chaos. I didn't know what I was doing half the time.

Annie Hogan: Lemmy from Motörhead was backstage; he brought out this massive knife straight after the gig with a massive line of speed on it all the way down to the handle. Well, I couldn't say no![22]

Less than a week later, Soft Cell returned for a tour of Spain that was to descend into outright chaos. The fact that nearly all recreational drugs were legal did not help matters. As Spain gradually reformed its legal system following the end of General Franco's dictatorship the previous decade, 1983 had seen the decriminalisation of all drugs for personal use, with no specifications on the quantities involved.[23]

Billy McGee: It was incredible, every gig we did people were tripping off their faces, breaking capsules of mescaline into their wine.

Gary Barnacle, Soft Cell saxophonist: I was a very straight person in that sense. I didn't even know the names of all the drugs. Mister Naive over here is going, 'How can Marc be so out of it after a few glasses of Spanish lager?'[24]

Dave Ball: I don't know why we even went to Spain. I think Marc thought of it as a working holiday, research for Marc and the Mambas. He tended to go through phases, he'd had this phase where he was into chanson, and now it happened to be Spain. There was one particular gig where we got there and the stage was dangerous. They had bullfights there so it was basically a big vat of blood with chipboard all over it. Our road crew told them it was too dangerous, that with the weight of the gear it would end up like a scene from *Carrie*. We said, 'We're not doing it'.[25]

We could go out to dinner but we're always on drugs

Billy McGee: We were staying in this really weird hotel, and we saw Marc downstairs in the foyer. He said, 'The gig's been pulled, it isn't safe, so let's go out'. We ended up sat on this boat all day drinking sangria, but then the tour manager found us and said, 'You've got to get down there now, they've got Stevo at gunpoint'. We'd all been drinking, we were still staggering about, but we went down there and weren't allowed out until Soft Cell paid them the money they were going to lose that night. They were working up the crowd outside, and said they were just going to feed us to them. I was so hammered I was going, 'Nah, they're not gonna do it', but the tour manager's saying, 'Honestly, this is actually happening'.

Gary Barnacle: Marc just had no chance of performing. He could barely speak, let alone remember all the words, but the next thing we know there were big heavies with guns, saying 'You will perform tonight, otherwise …', and they'd tap their guns.

Dave Ball: These people who were running it were holding us hostage. I think we ended up giving them about ten grand to buy our way out of it.[26]

Stevo: In my experience it was a nightmare. You could be put into a cell until you were proven innocent, but I was told that could take three or four days. I thought, 'What, am I going to cancel the rest of the tour because they're all in the nick?'[27]

Eventually, a van was brought around to the back of the venue, and the musicians were told to lay down in the back and cover themselves in blankets.

Billy McGee: We sped out of the venue with the crowd banging on the side of the van, screaming, crying and laughing hysterically all at the same time.

Martin McCarrick: At the end of my third year, I was called into the principal's office and told, 'You're not really committed to this course, are you?' We came to a compromise where I would commit to the course. I just did all the outside work without telling them.

Live performances that did take place found Soft Cell firing on all cylinders, playing on both sides of the thin line between transcendence and disaster as they continued through Spain and then a further run of summer shows in the UK.

Billy McGee: One night, I think it was in Valencia, somebody started spitting at Marc because he thought it was a punk gig. Dave picked up the bass guitar like it was a hammer and stepped out to the front of the stage, dark rings of black mascara down his face, beckoning the fan towards him with a weird smile on his face. The guy just crumpled and started crying.

Not content with just Soft Cell and the Mambas, Almond had also contributed lyrics and performance for Psychic TV's debut LP, *Force the Hand of Chance*, the previous year, and in between tour dates took part in an art piece with the band's John Gosling and Coil's Jhonn Balance, in which he performed a reading about drug-induced self-destruction while Gosling and Balance urinated and defecated behind him. It was enough to startle even Nick Cave, who was sat in the audience.[28] In another short-lived project with JG Thirlwell called Bruise n' Chain, Almond also opened for Cabaret Voltaire, and then together with Cave and Lydia Lunch they formed yet another group, this time titled the Immaculate Consumptive.

Marc Almond speaking to *NME*, 12 November 1983: I mean, ever since Soft Cell people have been telling me I've been making all the wrong moves, that I'm not playing by the rules, but to me success is being able to do something like the Immaculate Consumptive. It means working with people from whom I get great feedback; it is valuable working with these people.[29]

Nick Cave speaking to *NME*, 12 November 1983: I see it more as being the collective personality given to us by a not over imaginative music press. They do tend to dwell on Marc, Lydia and I being a complete misery guts. That's one common bond between us, I suppose.[30]

JG Thirlwell: Marc was always omnivorous and so was Lydia. And me, I need a lot of different avenues for what I do because there's no one project that's big enough for all of my ideas.

Lydia Lunch: Marc Almond, beautifully perverse, sweet beyond belief and dedicated to a unique form of expression all his own. Every moment spent with him was a glorious example of a passionate individual executing exactly what he was put on this earth to do: bless us with his presence. I adore.[31]

Lunch had been offered some shows at Danceteria to mark the Halloween of 1983, so proposed to Thirlwell, Almond and Cave that they do something together.

JG Thirlwell: We went about figuring out what the hell we were going to do, which consisted of putting together a backing track on a cassette for us to play live instruments over.

Billy McGee: Me, Annie and Martin worked on the backing tracks. Again, it was all late-night stuff. Nick Cave was on the floor, scribbling away in his notebook. Then he said, 'Can I start with just the double-bass player?', so I went into a room with him, him going through his lyrics while I was playing bass. I put down a bassline, then he started adding piano and all these other things. He was incredibly intense. Then they went off to tour the Eastern Seaboard.

JG Thirlwell: The show began with Lydia doing a couple of songs while I played sax, then me and Lydia doing a version of the Alice Cooper song 'Blue Turk' as a duet. Marc did some songs, I did a couple of Foetus songs, we did a version of [the Mambas'] 'A Million Manias'. Nick did a version of 'In the Ghetto', just piano and voice, then a version of 'A Box for Black Paul'. He never finished that fucking song. We played twice in New York and once at the 9:30 Club in Washington DC, and every time he would stop after five minutes and say, 'Yeah, well, it goes on like that for a bit longer'. It meant that the show just dribbled off. It was crazy.

We could go out to dinner but we're always on drugs

Billy McGee: It was at a time when Nick was in a dark place with heroin, Foetus was really into alcohol and speed. Marc was caught between all of that.

Immediately after the Immaculate Consumptive, Soft Cell rolled onwards into North America. It would be their first and only run of consistent shows across the continent, and though they did not know it, their last tour that century. In San Francisco they were greeted with rapture by the city's sizable gay scene. In Los Angeles, after a day spent huffing ethyl chloride from a rag as he was driven around on a sight-seeing tour in a bright red sportscar, one of three sold-out shows at the famous Palace Theatre ended with Almond tripping over a monitor and knocking himself unconscious.[32]

Billy McGee: Marc would really use the stage, running around all over the place. One night he suddenly collapsed at the end of the concert, and we'd thought he'd died.

Michael Jackson, still riding high following his multi-record-breaking smash hit *Thriller*, watched from the wings, reportedly impressed by what he witnessed.[33]

Chaotic as they were, the group were now operating at the peak of their powers as a live collective. 'Tainted Love' long since stricken from their setlist, they pushed deeper into the dark side of Soft Cell that had always existed in its shadow, powered by a reckless and relentless intake of amphetamines. Naturally, it could not last. Within just a few months, both the Mambas and Soft Cell were to implode.

Dave Ball: There was the pressure of being in Soft Cell, and the pressure of over-indulgence with various chemicals. We were both getting very involved in class-A substance abuse, seven days a week, and there's our crazy manager who doesn't say, 'Why don't you just go on holiday, take six months out, don't do any drugs, clean your act up and then come back refreshed?' We had a guy who was just as bad as we were! The whole thing became an endless party that was getting out of control.[34]

Heroin had been gradually taking hold over the scene. Almond started using after being introduced to the drug by an office assistant and addict named Stuart, only stopping after Stuart was arrested for possession. Ball, meanwhile, was ploughing an equally manic furrow in his own nascent solo career. Drawing too on Soft Cell's increasing association with Some Bizzare's left-field roster, he began producing for the likes of Cabaret Voltaire and playing on their album *The Crackdown*, and recorded the critically dismissed, if under-appreciated, album *In Strict Tempo*, for which Genesis P-Orridge and Virgin Prunes' Gavin Friday (who he was also to go on to produce) were enlisted as guest vocalists. He also scored a production of the Tennessee Williams play *Suddenly, Last Summer*, financed the entire project and hired Huw Feather as set designer.

Dave Ball: I was a manic workaholic, fuelled mostly by amphetamines, cocaine and black coffee, living on a multivitamin pill and a Mars a day – not exactly work, rest and play. I was very underweight and sometimes didn't sleep for five days at a time. With that amount of sleep deprivation I'd usually start hallucinating by day four, so with the aid of a few strong spliffs and a bottle or two of white wine I'd finally crash out and go into a semi-comatose state for about eighteen hours.[35]

The Mambas' second album, *Torment and Toreros*, received generally positive reviews. One, however, was particularly brutal.

Record Mirror, 13 August 1983: I don't know whether Marc regards his work with the Mambas as a bit of light relief away from the serious business of making money, but it sounds like that. *Torment and Toreros* is haaaard going, four sides of ill-disciplined doodling. It deals with familiar Almond obsessions: i.e., the generally scabrous side of life. I'm afraid I find Marc's murky travelogues neither outrageous nor daring but simply tedious [...] I'm sure they had a great time in the studio and really, they should have left it at that. Like all those people who mistake black leather and studded belts for some sort of decadent mean machine, Mr Almond has mistaken his own pop stature for divine inspiration. A fine performer, his tales are tired and his melody belongs to Davey.[36]

Dave Ball: Marc's response was to go to their offices, get out a bull whip and lash the editor. Which is ... not your normal relationship with the press.[37]

Anne Stephenson: He was so upset when he read the review that he just started raging, saying he was going to get his whip and go down there. Everyone was saying, 'You'd better not', but I don't think we thought he'd actually do it. He grabbed his bullwhip and went flying down there. We had all worked so bloody hard on that album, and it was good. We were hurt and upset too. It was a classic album; I'd never heard anything like it. I once said, 'I think we're making history in the studio at the moment'. And there's someone trashing it in the press, who had absolutely no idea what he was talking about.

Record Mirror, 20 August 1983: It all started when [Jim] Reid's purple prose landed on the Almond black leather sofa and burned a hole through to the carpet. A small dark streak was spotted careering through the streets of Soho and, seconds later, the foaming frothing heap of rage arrived at Jim's desk and throat. 'You're not fit to review my album,' Almond screamed, while lashing at the mild-mannered reporter with his favourite specially imported Zambian rhino whip. 'You got a grudge against me? I'll give you something to have a grudge about. I've lost friends and money making this album. I've made myself ill. You write anything else about me and you're a dead man!' And with that, the black tornado hurtled back to the studios where he and David Ball are putting down tracks for what was to be the forthcoming Soft Cell album.[38]

The story was picked up on by other publications, skewed into more dramatic retellings. One unfortunate writer, who compared being whipped by the diminutive Almond to being stroked by a mascara brush, found herself at the end of an abusive telegram in which he compared her to a 'gargantuan blancmange'.[39] At breaking point, without the consultation of those close to him, Almond then put out a statement to the press announcing his immediate retirement.

We could go out to dinner but we're always on drugs

Marc Almond, Some Bizzare press statement, August 1983:
Finding myself increasingly confused and unhappy within
the music business I no longer wish to continue on the
recording side of the music scene, whatever that may be,
and whoever I may be. The Mambas no longer exist and
the finishing of the new Soft Cell album, currently being
recorded, is in doubt. I no longer wish to sing on records, in
fact, I no longer wish to sing. I don't want to be involved in
any more interviews – this is no disrespect, or show of petty
arrogance, to those that have written constructively, fairly
and favourably about me – there are those whose writing
I respect and also whose friendship I respect, that will continue, I hope – to those on the other side of the fence – go
to hell! I don't seek praise or glorification, I just seek con-
structive and fair critique, though whenever I get praise, I
feel confused and filled with self-doubt – one of my major
problems at the moment – the bad things I'm afraid I take to
heart – that's my problem. If there are any future recordings,
there will be extremely few if any, which will come as a great
relief to those who find my singing a pain to the ears. I don't
know about my future, but it could possibly involve working
on the other side of the Some Bizzare fence working for
other bands – on the invisible side. I may however continue
some live work of some form which I enjoy, but not under
Mambas or Soft Cell guises and it is unlikely they will be
at all commercial, though commitments abroad will have to
be fulfilled. To the fans that have supported me I hope they
will understand my reasons and to keep their ears open for
anything I may do. Thanks to those who have supported
me – confused? Not half as much as I am.[40]

211

Billy McGee: Steve Sherlock phoned me up at home and said, 'Have you seen the news? Soft Cell and the Mambas have split up!' I just thought well, that was short lived.

Colin Bell: I don't know how seriously we would have taken it. The record company certainly wouldn't have taken it as gospel.

Anne Stephenson: Marc had a vulnerable side. I remember going into the kitchen at Stevo's house and I heard someone just sobbing in the dark. It was Marc, just crying his eyes out. Just absolutely empty. He had poured out his heart and soul non-stop for a week in the studio. He was exhausted. There was nothing left. My heart bled seeing him so wrecked. I was shocked. I had never seen anything like it before in my life.

In the days following his announcement, Almond came to regret his haste. Calling into BBC Radio 1 DJ David 'Kid' Jensen after he heard him mention the retirement live on air, he proclaimed that he was unretiring just as swiftly. The following day, he leaned out of the balcony of Trident House and announced his resurrection once more to the still-despairing Gutterhearts gathered below, throwing down black silk roses.

Stevo, speaking to *Record Mirror*, 20 August 1983: The end is when Marc and David and I say it is the end. They will be finishing the album – the songs are too good to let them go […] The Marc and the Mambas split is official. They were becoming a commodity and that's not how it started. It started as an outlet. One of the great things about Marc Almond is that he does reveal himself and that's why everything is so personal. At the end of the day, I will stick by what he says. He should be loyal to himself and not a commodity.[41]

Marc Almond, speaking to *NME*, 12 November 1983: I don't care if people slag my work off, but if you're going to slam it, please be witty. How dare anyone criticise someone else if they're going to be dull about it![42]

The Mambas did pick up for two final gigs: a show at the Duke of York's Theatre, supported by a cabaret of vaudeville performers, flamenco dancers and a Balkan folk group, as well as for a one-off appearance in Tel Aviv.

Billy McGee: When we did theatres, that was when everything just came together. What Marc was always saying was we're not rock and roll, that we weren't going be a band that goes out and does a six-month tour of three days on, one day off, stuck on a tour bus. Marc wanted to go off and adventure, do something new and adventure. We always used to say, 'Wouldn't it be great if we were just a travelling theatre group?' To go to a city, stay for two weeks, play every night then go to the next, that would have been fantastic.

Anne Stephenson: We thought Tel Aviv was really exciting. I got to go on a camel, and being a bit of a Catholic I was determined to go and see where Jesus was born in Bethlehem. There was just a plastic doll stuck in a hole in the ground – that was supposed to be it!

For Soft Cell, however, the damage had been done. Ball, too, was exhausted, and drawn more and more towards production and behind-the-scenes work rather than relentless touring. He had also announced his engagement to Gini while on Soft Cell's Spanish tour, and was soon to become a father for the first time. They declined the offer to tour Japan the following year.

Stevo: I remember saying to them, you should keep Soft Cell going. If you've got a band as big as Soft Cell, who in their right mind would want to lose it?[43]

Dave Ball: It was a good move to stop when we did. I'd just become a father and got married and that wasn't really conducive to the life I had been embarking on. We decided to make one more album, do some final shows, then call it a day.[44]

That album was to be titled *This Last Night ... In Sodom*, and if the darkness had been ramped up on *The Art of Falling Apart*, here it was to consume Soft Cell's sound entirely. For the album's artwork they eschewed the delicately poised tableaus of its predecessors in favour of a scrawled image by a child suffering from severe schizophrenia that Almond had found in a textbook about insanity. 'Meet Murder, My Angel' portrays a twisted figure who views killing their lover as the purest expression of adoration, while 'The Best Way to Kill' recounts a ghoulish tabloid feature in which readers were asked to vote for their favourite method of execution. 'Slave to This' melts down entirely, vocals layered on top of one another as the babblings of a God-obsessed madman tangle with sweeping melodramatic pronouncements that vow revenge on those who've transgressed. 'L'Esqualita' was written in tribute to the famous Puerto Rican drag club they'd frequented in New York, and appropriated a comment first uttered by Nick Cave's partner and collaborator Anita Lane during the Immaculate Consumptive dates that accurately summed up the era: 'We could go out to dinner, but we're always on drugs.'

Ball produced the record himself, recording in mono as a tribute to the maverick Phil Spector. Holed up in the Pink Floyd-owned Britannia Row Studios, the only additional personnel were Gini Ball and Gary Barnacle. No longer paying lip service to synth pop, and with Phonogram past caring, this was to be their vision alone, a radical collage of sounds more in line with Foetus and Psychic TV than 'Tainted Love'.

Dave Ball: It was the sound of self-destruction, as the song 'Mr. Self Destruct' kind of implies. A crash, more than a bang I suppose.[45]

Annie Hogan: It had all started falling apart, after *The Art of Falling Apart*, and *This Last Night ... In Sodom* was the sound of burnout in full sonic splendour. It's a shame that they didn't go on from there, but it was their final meltdown.[46]

Gary Barnacle: It was really well-recorded, really powerful stuff. I think it's one of their best moments. It's slipped under the radar because they weren't available to promote it and the record company didn't really put much behind it. I think they probably thought to themselves, 'The loyal fans are gonna buy it anyway, that's enough to make it a worthwhile exercise, but not to go over and above to get it out there.'

By the time *This Last Night … In Sodom* was released on 1 March 1984, the band was no more. Its two singles troubled the charts – the emotionally explosive 'Soul Inside', its poppiest moment, had reached number sixteen the previous autumn, and a gloriously lopsided cover of Jack Hammer's 1960s R&B track 'Down in the Subway' got to number twenty-four in February. Reviews ranged from the glowing to the outright hostile, not least from Soft Cell's old foe Paul Morley at *NME*.

Melody Maker, 17 March 1984: Most of *This Last Night* sounds like it was torn straight from Dave Ball's notebook, rush-mixed and crash-edited by slavering degenerates, and passionately sung by a chained-up dwarf with violent palpitations. Par for the course, then.[47]

Sounds, 24 March 1984: All good things must come to an end, it seems, but Soft Cell's final curtain is no flimsy drape, no throwaway tinselled trivia for 'the fans'. It's a dark and heavy weave with some ugly living truths trapped in its shadowy folds.[48]

NME, 17 March 1984: This LP is a shambles. It sounds like it might have taken thirty-seven minutes to record. Lucy tells me it took five months, during which Marc quit at least three times. What a fragile little brat. That might be the nicest thing I say about him in this review. I might not even mention that odd Ball figure […] Piss off Soft Cell. So say all of us. So say Almond and Ball. By the sound of this.[49]

We could go out to dinner but we're always on drugs

This time, however, there would be no revenge taken, no bullwhip attack or abusive telegram. Nor were there any interviews to promote the record. There had not even been much of a fallout between Almond and Ball, rather an amicably arranged hiatus that was to last until the new millennium. Almond moved onto a new project, the Willing Sinners, and a solo career that sprawled off in every direction. Ball, unceremoniously dropped by Phonogram but still backed by Some Bizzare, focussed on production and formed a series of short-lived projects before the Grid, a partnership with another Psychic TV collaborator, Richard Norris, returned him to mainstream success with a string of dance hits in the 1990s. The first phase of Soft Cell had simply faded out.

This alone, of course, would not have been befitting of a group so drawn to drama. In January 1984, two months before *This Last Night … In Sodom*, Soft Cell arranged two final shows at the Hammersmith Palais in which to revel in it all. Perhaps tellingly, recollections of the show are thin on fine details, remembered as if through a haze.

Melody Maker, 21 January 1984: Soft Cell's last night in Sodom, staged suitably at the lurid and uncomfortable Palais, was a diffuse mix of abandon and throwaway lines, a kind of passionate indifference. I couldn't be sure if it was any good or not, but it was an event […] The Cell's songs tended to merge into one giant smear of noise, all thundering drum machine and a bass sound like dead lumberjacks falling into a swamp.[50]

Marc Almond: It should have been time for a crowning triumph, not for a sad farewell. We had both finally become the live act we had always aspired to be, and were at last making the records we wanted to. What we needed more than anything was for someone to make us see sense, to sit us down and explain to us from a bold business point of view just what we had.[51]

Billy McGee: I was at the show, but I wasn't performing. I just remember thinking, 'God, were we really this loud?' It was thunderous.

Gini Ball: I was eight months pregnant. Someone was saying to me backstage, 'What are you doing here?' Maybe they thought I would have been better off sitting at home.

Dave Ball: There were a lot of people weeping, a lot of people crying. It was very emotional, very intense. People really did think, 'Oh, that's it. That's farewell.' I think Marc enjoyed the emotion of a farewell gig, the waves of emotion that you get.[52]

Gary Barnacle Those gigs were amazing. The fans knew that it was the last one. It was powerful stuff. I've never played with a band like it where there's no normal rhythm section, and I was the only instrument that was free. Ironically, this electronic pop duo gave me the most freedom to express myself I've ever had.

The set spanned their career, from the futurist proto-rave of 'Memorabilia' to the provincial claustrophobia of 'Bedsitter', the sublime sorrow of 'Say Hello, Wave Goodbye' to the

gothic excess of 'Martin', to almost half of *This Last Night …
In Sodom*'s glorious implosion. They still, however, refused
to play 'Tainted Love'.

Dave Ball: I didn't really feel anything. I'd had so much coke, I
couldn't even feel my nose.[53]

EPILOGUE

It could all have been so different. Had Soft Cell a less antagonistic relationship with Phonogram, plus a properly organised touring schedule rather than a mishmash of inter-tangled side projects that saw them lurch from Spain to Tel Aviv, they might not have screeched to a halt with those two triumphant shows in Hammersmith in 1984.

Consider Depeche Mode, Soft Cell's fellow stars of the *Some Bizzare Album*, whose methodical touring, consistent progression in the studio and skilful negotiation of line-up changes had them playing American arenas by the end of the decade and making their way to their own dark masterpiece *Violator* in 1990 without the fit of mental collapse Soft Cell experienced with *This Last Night … In Sodom*. The Human League, whose 'Love Action (I Believe in Love)' was the only real contender that 'Tainted Love' faced for the definitive British pop single of 1981, rode out tumultuous intra-band relationships to release consistently throughout the 1980s, 1990s and beyond – albeit to diminishing returns.

There were real human costs to the hedonism that Soft Cell, their friends, colleagues, hangers-on and bandmates experienced, an aftermath to the drug-taking that quickly progressed from thrilling to something altogether more insidious, and to the frayed interpersonal relationships that have left lasting fallouts. The immense pressure that ultimately led to Soft Cell's end might have been channelled into a dark masterpiece in the form of *This Last Night ... In Sodom*, but as *Non-Stop Erotic Cabaret*'s incisive mixture of flamboyance and social observation proves, there is more than one way to make a great album; the idea that great art can only be borne of suffering is toxic and untrue.

Had Soft Cell simply arrived a little later, perhaps in an era less hostile to queerness in pop, the tabloids and paparazzi might not have dogged them with such ferocity. Were they among the crop of projects like Yazoo, Eurythmics and Pet Shop Boys, for whom the concept of an electronic duo was an established format, rather than a line-up that would see record companies scrambling, there might have been something resembling a map. Had they never released 'Tainted Love' at all, or had it not struck whatever strange chord that it did in 1981, they might well have continued to plough their experimental furrow as the acclaimed, uncommercial cult heroes that they had aimed to be in the first place.

If there was one quality that defined Soft Cell from the off, however, that they had in more abundance than any of their contemporaries, it was restlessness. It was restlessness that saw their voracious cultural appetite absorb everything from Weimar expressionism to Northern Soul during their formative years in Leeds, that led them into every flavour of New York club and Soho dive, seeking out their most extreme corners instead of skating across these cities' surfaces, and made the Mambas into the sprawl of exotic sonics that it was. No single framework was ever going to be enough for them to satisfactorily express what they collaged out of this cornucopia of different influences, and similarly, their career was never realistically going to settle into one single 'pathway'. Instead, they were always destined to flitter between surprise pop stardom and their avant-garde roots, their career pock-marked with the craters made when one world collided with the other – most notably when the 'Sex Dwarf' video, essentially a performance art piece akin to Almond's Leeds shows, was met with the opinions of a Thatcher-electing general public via the tabloid press.

For all the animosity they received, Phonogram were in fact relatively tame in their attempts to guide Soft Cell towards a happy medium; by the standards of other record companies of the time they were benign in their intentions. Yet Soft Cell's real genius was their refusal to water things down, and to insist that their music maintain all the sharp edges and messy boundaries that made it brilliant. In Stevo, they found a figure so anarchic that he created ample diversion for them to do so. There is of course a substantial argument to be made that Some Bizzare only hastened Soft Cell's demise, Stevo pouring canisters of petrol on the fires that a manager's job description demands he should extinguish. Yet purely in terms of what Soft Cell achieved in a mere three years between the *Some Bizzare Album* and *This Last Night ... In Sodom*, his peculiar brilliance cannot be denied. Chaotic as it was, Some Bizzare provided an atmosphere in which Soft Cell could briefly thrive, the greenhouse in which they could grow into the exotic, luxuriant, almost certainly toxic flower which, though it only bloomed briefly, bloomed with a brilliance rarely witnessed.

ACKNOWLEDGEMENTS

There are a number of people without whom this book would not exist at all. My partner Sarah Cohen is foremost among them. Her endless well of patience, astute proofreading, encouragement to push myself creatively and extreme capacity for moral support have kept me going, not only through the process of this book and the multiple crises of confidence that it has elicited, but every day since we met. Adelle Stripe, who not only provided my model for how best to write a book about music, but whose enthusiasm for an article I wrote about Soft Cell for the *Quietus* was what led me on the path to it getting published; such displays of faith in my writing, not least from those whose work I admire so much, have been few and far between, and I appreciate it more than I can say.

That initial article was written under the sage editorship of John Doran, for whom I have to thank for my first paid job as a music journalist, and for helping hone my craft over the course of the decade I have written for the site. The same can be said for Luke Turner, to whom I am grateful for the guidance he offered when I first began writing a book.

Acknowledgements

It was also at the *Quietus* where I met Anna Wood, whose mentorship was of colossal importance to me as a young writer, and whose friendship remains similarly valuable to me to this day.

I would also like to thank my parents, Peter and Katie Clarke, and my brother Doug, for providing an environment when I was growing up where creativity was always prided above all else, where my teenage creative whims (not least of being a music writer) were always taken seriously, where exposure to art was of paramount importance, and where getting on the blag was actively encouraged. The Cohen family, too – Gail, Graham, Anna and Luna – for providing hospitality, humour, encouragement and, on multiple occasions, a place to live.

As I finalised the first draft of this book, tidying up my references and going through all of those who were kind enough to agree to an interview, it struck me just how many people the actual contents of this book have relied upon, and how many favours I now owe. In almost every case, not only were interviewees generous with their time and thoughtful in their answers, but also willing to suggest others I should speak to.

Particular thanks must go to Dave Ball, Annie Hogan, Peter Ashworth, Jose Warden and Brian Moss for agreeing to be interviewed more than once. Annie, in particular, made heroic efforts in terms of tracking down further interviewees. Similarly, Debbie Ball of Create Spark PR went above and beyond on multiple occasions when it came to my communication with Soft Cell themselves, as did Chris Smith and Mark Langthorne. And to all at the Manchester University Press, particularly Douglas Field, Emma Brennan and Alun Richards.

Acknowledgements

And of course, in no particular order, all of my friends from Liverpool to London to Cardiff to Australia and beyond: Tom Davies, Mark Rhodes, Jess Plummer, Polly Foreman, Lisa Fawcett, Tom Davis-Costerton, Megan De Meo, Charlotte Brookhouse, Charlie Bollaan, Holly Watkin, Katrina Lamming, Leo Watkins, Charlie Daniels (aka David Manning, aka Pascal Limon), Tom Murphy, Tim Yates and Sian Wakeley.

NOTES

1 Lubbock's Day

1 Janice Formichella, 'Victorian gloves: etiquette for use', *Recollections* (blog), 10 January 2021, https://www.recollections.biz/blog/victorian-gloves-etiquette-for-use [accessed 16 August 2023].

2 Interview with the author, 17 August 2022. Includes all subsequent quotes from Dr Kathryn Ferry.

3 Interview with the author, 9 November 2021. Parts of this interview formed the basis of Patrick Clarke, 'Non-Stop Erotic Cabaret: an oral history of Soft Cell's debut album', *The Quietus*, 26 November 2021, https://www.thequietus.com/articles/30878-soft-cell-non-stop-erotic-cabaret-oral-history-dave-ball-marc-almond-interview [accessed 16 August 2023].

4 Interview with the author, 11 November 2021. Parts of this interview formed the basis of Clarke, 'Non-Stop Erotic Cabaret'.

5 Neil Taylor and J. Christopher Holloway, *The Business of Tourism*, 7th edn (Hoboken, NJ: Financial Times/Prentice Hall, 2006), p. 29.

6 Alan Fowler, *Lancashire Cotton Operatives and Work, 1900–1950* (Farnham: Ashgate, 2003), p. 63.

7 Horace G. Hutchinson, *Life of Sir John Lubbock* (London: Macmillan and Co., 1914), pp. 122–4.

8 'History', Brighton & Hove Museums, https://brightonmuseums.org.uk/visit/royal-pavilion-garden/our-history/ [accessed 15 August 2023].

9 Interview with the author, 2 June 2023.

10 Interview with the author, 14 June 2023. Includes all subsequent quotes from Huw Feather.

11 Interview with the author, 9 November 2021.

12 'Blackpool Tower vs Eiffel Tower', The Blackpool Tower, 9 January 2023, https://www.theblackpooltower.com/news/blackpool-tow er-vs-eiffel-tower [accessed 15 August 2023].

13 Interview with the author, 12 June 2023.

14 Interview with the author, 30 August 2022. Includes all subse-quent quotes from Norman Barrett.

15 Interview with the author, 2 June 2023.

16 Interview with the author, 30 August 2022.

17 Marc Almond, *Tainted Life* (London: Pan Macmillan, 2000), p. 44.

18 Interview with the author, 29 August 2022.

19 Interview with the author, 11 November 2021.

20 Interview with the author, 2 June 2023.

21 *Ibid.*

22 Interview with the author, 12 June 2023.

23 Interview with the author, 16 August 2022.

24 Almond, *Tainted Life*, p. 36.

25 Interview with the author, 11 November 2021.

2 The Yorkshire Vortex

1 Elena Crippa and Beth Williamson, *Basic Design* (London: Tate, 2013), p. 8.

2 *Ibid.*

3 Gavin Butt, *No Machos or Pop Stars: When the Leeds Art Experiment Went Punk* (Durham, NC: Duke University Press, 2022), p. 12.

4 Patrick Heron, 'Murder of the art schools', *Guardian*, 12 October 1971, p. 8.

5 William Coldstream, *First Report of the National Advisory Council on Art Education* (London: HM Stationery Office, 1960).

6 '170 years of Leeds College of Art 1846–2016', Leeds College of Art, https://web.archive.org/web/20170916002407/http:// www.leeds-art.ac.uk/alumni/170-years-of-leeds-college-of-art-1846-2016 [accessed 15 August 2023].

Notes

7 Interview with the author, 5 April 2023. Includes all subsequent quotes from Geoff Teasdale.

8 Jeff Nuttall, *Performance Art: Memoirs* (London: Calder, 1979), p. 69.

9 Interview with the author, 22 February 2023. Includes all subsequent quotes from James Charnley.

10 Jeff Nuttall, *Bomb Culture: 50th Anniversary Edition* (London: Strange Attractor, 2019).

11 *Ibid.*, p. 5

12 Interview with the author, 27 February 2023. Includes all subsequent quotes from Anne Tilby.

13 Interview with the author, 10 February 2023.

14 Interview with the author, 13 February 2023. Includes all subsequent quotes from Sophie Parkin.

15 Interview with the author, 2 June 2023.

16 Quoted in Neil Cooper, 'Marc Almond – Ten Plagues', *Herald*, 19 July 2011.

17 Almond, *Tainted Life,* p. 61.

18 Butt, *No Machos or Pop Stars*, p. 176.

19 'Birds lives saved by attack', *Daily Telegraph*, 17 November 1976, p. 19.

20 'Budgie killers had to flee from angry audience', *Daily Telegraph*, 27 May 1977, p. 3.

21 *Ibid.*

22 Almond, *Tainted Life*, p. 65.

23 Interview with the author, 12 June 2023.

24 Interview with the author, 3 March 2023. Includes all subsequent quotes from Hugo Burnham.

25 Interview with the author, 23 March 2023.

26 Almond, *Tainted Life*, p. 76.

27 Interview with the author, 11 November 2021.

28 David Cleall, 'John Bull Puncture Repair Kit', *Unfinished Histories: Recording the History of Alternative Theatre*, https://www.unfinishedhistories.com/history/companies/john-bull-puncture-repair-kit [accessed 29 August 2023].

29 Interview with the author, 2 June 2023.

30 Trevor Pinch and Frank Trocco, *Analog Days: The Invention and Impact of the Moog Synthesizer* (Cambridge, MA: Harvard University Press, 2004).

Notes

31 Interview with the author, 2 June 2023.
32 Simon Ford, *Wreckers of Civilisation: The Story of COUM Transmissions and Throbbing Gristle* (London: Black Dog Publishing, 2017), section 6, p. 28.
33 Thompson Prentice, 'Adults only art show angers an MP', *Daily Mail*, 19 October 1976, p. 17.
34 Almond, *Tainted Life*, p. 85.
35 Interview with the author, 11 November 2021.
36 Interview with the author, 1 February 2023. Includes all subsequent quotes from John Keenan.
37 Interview with the author, 12 November 2021. Parts of this interview formed the basis of Clarke, 'Non-Stop Erotic Cabaret'.
38 Interview with the author, 12 June 2023.
39 Interview with the author, 14 February 2023. Includes all subsequent quotes from Chris Neate.
40 Marcel Anders, 'How David Bowie and Jacques Brel shaped Soft Cell', Red Bull, 16 May 2022, https://www.redbull.com/gb-en/theredbulletin/playlist-soft-cell-influences-marc-almond-interview [accessed 27 August 2023].
41 Thomas Barrett, 'First Damn Yankee owner reflects on "phenomenal" early years in 1970s', *Stray Ferret*, 11 June 2021, https://thestrayferret.co.uk/first-damn-yankee-owner-reflects-on-phenomenal-early-years-in-1970s [accessed 29 August 2023].
42 Interview with the author, 19 April 2023. Includes all subsequent quotes from Dino Wiand.
43 Interview with the author, 23 March 2023.
44 Interview with the author, 7 July 2023. Includes all subsequent quotes from Ian Dewhirst.
45 James is not to be confused with the later BBC DJ of the same name.
46 Interview with the author, 23 March 2023.
47 Interview with the author, 22 March 2023. Includes all subsequent quotes from Brian Moss.
48 Butt, *No Machos or Pop Stars*, p. 5.
49 '£395 arts grant for balancing pole', *Daily Telegraph*, 12 March 1976, p. 19.
50 Almond, *Tainted Life*, p. 71.
51 Interview with the author, 23 March 2023.

52 Gordon Burn, *Somebody's Husband, Somebody's Son: The Story of the Yorkshire Ripper* (London: Faber & Faber, 2004).
53 Interview with the author, 12 June 2023.

3 Memorabilia

1 Jon Welch, 'Sex Pistols: anarchy in the UK and the tour they tried to ban', BBC News, 3 December 2016, https://www.bbc.co.uk/news/uk-england-norfolk-38165091 [accessed 16 August 2023].
2 Patrick Clarke, 'It's the buzz, cock! Spiral Scratch 40 years on', *The Quietus*, 30 January 2017, https://thequietus.com/articles/21653-buzzcocks-interview-spiral-scratch-anniversary-review [accessed 16 August 2023].
3 *Ibid.*
4 Interview with the author, 2 June 2023.
5 *Ibid.*
6 *Ibid.*
7 Interview with the author, 29 March 2023.
8 Interview with the author, 12 June 2023.
9 Interview with the author, 23 March 2023.
10 Interview with the author, 29 March 2023.
11 Interview with the author, 23 March 2023.
12 Paul Morley, 'The squalor show goes on', *New Musical Express*, 20 September 1980, p. 48.
13 Betty Page [Beverley Glick], 'Soft Cell: sweet cell music', *Sounds*, 21 March 1981.
14 Interview with the author, 24 August 2023. Includes all subsequent quotes from Steve Parry.
15 Dave Simpson, 'Gary Numan and Mary Vango: how we made Are "Friends" Electric?', *Guardian*, 18 February 2014, https://www.theguardian.com/music/2014/feb/18/how-we-made-are-friends-electric-gary-numan [accessed 16 August 2023].
16 Peter Nash, *The Human League* (London: W.H. Allen, 1982).
17 Interview with the author, 12 June 2023.
18 'Interview with Andrew Fletcher', *modefan.com*, 1 February 2011, https://modefan.com/interview-andrew-fletcher/ [accessed 17 August 2023].

Notes

19 Interview with the author, 12 November 2021. Includes all subsequent quotes from Daniel Miller.
20 Interview with the author, 5 June 2023. Includes all subsequent quotes from Darla-Jane Gilroy.
21 Interview with the author, 23 May 2023. Includes all subsequent quotes from Rusty Egan.
22 *Blitzed!* [film], dir. Bruce Ashley and Michael Donald (London: Beyond TNC, 2020).
23 Nick Rhodes, 'How we opened the door to the 1980s', *Daily Telegraph*, 22 April 2006, https://www.telegraph.co.uk/culture/music/rockandjazzmusic/3651745/How-we-opened-the-door-to-the-1980s.html [accessed 16 August 2023].
24 Interview with the author, 26 May 2023. Includes all subsequent quotes from Richard Strange.
25 Robin Deneslow, 'Cabaret gets even more decadent', *Guardian*, 15 January 1981.

4 Art terrorism

1 Interview with the author, 30 August 2023.
2 Interview with the author, 6 June 2023. Includes all subsequent quotes from Beverley Glick.
3 Interview with the author, 30 August 2023.
4 Interview with the author, 2 June 2023.
5 Interview with the author, 30 August 2023.
6 Interview with the author, 9 November 2021.
7 Interview with the author, 12 June 2023.
8 *Ibid.*
9 Quoted in Johnny Rogan, *Starmakers and Svengalis: The History of British Pop Management* (Philadelphia, PA: Trans-Atlantic Publications, 1988), p. 263.
10 Interview with the author, 23 March 2023.
11 Interview with the author, 11 November 2021. Parts of this interview formed the basis of Clarke, 'Non-Stop Erotic Cabaret'.
12 Interview with the author, 11 November 2021.
13 Interview with the author, 9 November 2021.
14 Interview with the author, 2 June 2023.
15 *Ibid.*
16 *Ibid.*

Notes

17 Interview with the author, 9 November 2021.
18 *Ibid.*
19 Interview with the author, 11 November 2021.

5 Da dun dun

1 Interview with the author, 12 June 2023.
2 *Northern Soul: Living for the Weekend* [film], dir. James Maycock (London: BBC, 2014).
3 Interview with the author, 30 June 2023. Includes all subsequent quotes from Ian Levine.
4 Interview with the author, 28 June 2023. Includes all subsequent quotes from Colin Curtis.
5 Interview with the author, 2 June 2023.
6 Top 2000 a gogo, 'Gloria Jones – Tainted Love | The Story Behind the Song | Top 2000 a gogo' [video], YouTube, 23 May 2018, https://www.youtube.com/watch?v=ViWAVwY7LtU [accessed 17 August 2023].
7 *Northern Soul: Living for the Weekend.*
8 Interview with the author, 11 November 2021.
9 Interview with the author, 9 November 2021.
10 Interview with the author, 11 November 2021.
11 Interview with the author, 24 November 2021. Parts of this interview formed the basis of Clarke, 'Non-Stop Erotic Cabaret'.
12 Interview with the author, 6 July 2023. Includes all subsequent quotes from Colin Bell.
13 Interview with the author, 19 July 2023.
14 Interview with the author, 21 April 2023.
15 Interview with the author, 24 November 2021.
16 Interview with the author, 23 March 2023.
17 Interview with the author, 29 March 2023.
18 Interview with the author, 23 March 2023.
19 Interview with the author, 9 March 2021.

6 *Top of the Pops*

1 Interview with the author, 23 March 2023.
2 Interview with the author, 7 June 2023. Includes all subsequent quotes from Ian Gittins.

Notes

3 Interview with the author, 3 August 2023. Includes all subsequent quotes from Roy Gould.

4 Interview with the author, 2 June 2023.

5 Interview with the author, 9 November 2021.

6 Interview with the author, 11 November 2021.

7 Interview with the author, 9 November 2021.

8 *Ibid.*

9 *Ibid.*

10 Interview with the author, 23 June 2023.

11 Interview with the author, 20 June 2023. Includes all subsequent quotes from Tim Arnold.

12 Interview with the author, 11 November 2023.

13 Interview with the author, 6 July 2023.

14 Interview with the author, 11 November 2021.

15 Interview with the author, 23 March 2023.

16 Interview with the author, 9 November 2021.

17 Interview with the author, 11 November 2021.

18 Interview with the author, 23 March 2023.

19 *Ibid.*

20 Kurt Loder, 'David Bowie: straight time', *Rolling Stone*, 12 May 1983.

21 Interview with the author, 11 November 2021.

22 Interview with the author, 9 November 2021.

23 Interview with the author, 23 March 2021.

24 Dave Ball, *Electronic Boy: My Life in and out of Soft Cell* (London: Omnibus Press, 2020), p. 125.

25 Interview with the author, 30 August 2023.

26 Interview with the author, 11 November 2021.

27 Interview with the author, 11 November 2021. Parts of this interview formed the basis of 'Non-Stop Erotic Cabaret: An Oral History of Soft Cell's Debut Album', *The Quietus*, 26 November 2021. Includes all subsequent quotes from Tim Pope.

28 Interview with the author, 29 March 2023.

29 Interview with the author, 11 November 2021.

30 Interview with the author, 9 November 2021.

31 Interview with the author, 11 November 2021.

32 *Ibid.*

7 I shook them up and I gave them hell

1 Daniel Dylan Wray, 'The story behind the "first ever ecstasy song"', *VICE*, 10 November 2021, https://www.vice.com/en/article/v7dmdd/soft-cell-memorabilia-anniver-first-ever-ecstasy-song [accessed 17 August 2023].

2 Interview with the author, 23 March 2023.

3 Interview with the author, 11 November 2021.

4 *Ibid.*

5 Interview with the author, 19 July 2023.

6 Interview with the author, 29 March 2023.

7 Interview with the author, 30 August 2023.

8 Interview with the author, 9 November 2021.

9 Interview with the author, 6 June 2023. Includes all subsequent quotes from Harvey Goldberg.

10 Interview with the author, 29 June 2023. Includes all subsequent quotes from Dianne Brill.

11 Interview with the author, 12 June 2023. Includes all subsequent quotes from Don Wershba.

12 Tim Lawrence, *Life and Death on the New York Dance Floor, 1980–1983* (Durham, NC: Duke University Press, 2016), pp. 1–5.

13 Interview with the author, 5 June 2023. Includes all subsequent quotes from Jack Fritscher.

14 Interview with the author, 6 August 2023. Includes all subsequent quotes from Richard Boch.

15 'Section 1: Trust in Government 1958–2010', Pew Research Center, 18 April 2010, https://www.pewresearch.org/politics/2010/04/18/section-1-trust-in-government-1958-2010 [accessed 18 August 2023].

16 Anthony Haden-Guest, *The Last Party: Studio 54, Disco, and the Culture of the Night* (New York: William Morrow, 1997), pp. 79–85.

17 Interview with the author, 27 July 2023. Includes all subsequent quotes from Pamina Brassey.

18 Interview with the author, 25 May 2023. Includes all subsequent quotes from Rudolf Piper.

19 Haden-Guest, *The Last Party*, pp. 197–210.

20 'CBGB is the undisputed birthplace of punk', CBGB & OMFUG, https://www.cbgb.com/about [accessed 18 August 2023].

Notes

21 Bill Brewster and Frank Broughton, *Last Night a DJ Saved My Life: The History of the Disc Jockey* (London: Headline, 2000), pp. 278–84.

22 Brewster and Broughton, *Last Night a DJ Saved My Life*, pp. 269–72

23 Anna Quindlen, 'Where to roller skate to a disco beat', *New York Times*, 20 March 1981.

24 'Kool Lady Blue reflects on the golden age of hip-hop and dance music', *Red Bull Music Academy Daily*, 14 February 2019, https://daily.redbullmusicacademy.com/2019/02/kool-lady-blue-interview [accessed 28 August 2023].

25 *Ibid.*

26 *Ibid.*

27 Interview with the author, 12 June 2023.

28 'The future is history: the birth of ZE Records', ZE Records, 25 August 2015, https://web.archive.org/web/20240106100007/https://www.zerecords.com/about.html [accessed 18 August 2023].

29 Amar Ediriwira, 'Something like a phenomenon: the complete 99 Records story', *Vinyl Factory*, 15 March 2015, https://thevinyl factory.com/features/something-like-a-phenomenon-the-complete-99-records-story/ [accessed 18 August 2023].

30 'Neil Cooper, 71, who founded a rock and reggae record label', *New York Times*, 23 August 2001.

31 Thomas Galdino, 'The story behind Sugarhill Gang's "Rapper's Delight"', *American Songwriter*, 1 May 2023, https://american songwriter.com/the-story-behind-sugarhill-gangs-rappers-delight/ [accessed 18 August 2023].

32 Tim Blank, 'Mudd quake', *New York Times Magazine*, 25 February 2001.

33 Brewster and Broughton, *Last Night a DJ Saved My Life*.

34 Michaelangelo Matos, 'Reflecting on a New York club scene D.J.', *New York Times*, 27 October 2015.

35 *Ibid.*

36 Interview with the author, 12 June 2023.

37 Interview with the author, 21 April 2023.

38 Jack Fritscher, *Profiles in Gay Courage: Leatherfolk, Arts, and Ideas* (Sonoma, CA: Palm Drive Publishing, 2022), p. 62.

39 Interview with the author, 2 June 2023.

40 *Ibid.*

41 Interview with the author, 12 June 2023.

42 Interview with the author, 9 November 2021.

43 Interview with the author, 19 July 2023.

44 Interview with the author, 21 April 2023.

45 Interview with the author, 12 June 2023.

46 Gavin Martin, 'It's silly celly time, kids', *New Musical Express*, 28 November 1981, p. 37.

47 Steve Sutherland, 'Cruel cabaret comedy', *Melody Maker*, 28 November 1981, p. 17.

48 Interview with the author, 9 November 2021.

49 'The story of the Human League's "Dare" and "Love and Dancing"', *Classic Album Sundays*, https://classicalbumsun days.com/classic-album-sundays-presents-human-league-dare/ [accessed 18 August 2023].

50 Ian Wade, 'Love & Ecstatic Dancing: Soft Cell & Human League go long', *The Quietus*, 22 June 2022, https://thequietus.com/ articles/31680-love-non-stop-ecstatic-dancing [accessed 18 August 2023].

51 Interview with the author, 19 July 2023.

52 Interview with the author, 11 November 2021.

8 Soho

1 Interview with the author, 9 November 2021.

2 Marc Almond, *Afterlife: In Search of the Pleasure Palace* (London: Pan Macmillan, 2004), p. 27.

3 Interview with the author, 3 August 2023.

4 Interview with the author, 12 June 2023.

5 *Ibid*.

6 Ken Roe, 'KOKO in London, GB', *Cinema Treasures*, https://cin ematreasures.org/theaters/14486 [accessed 18 August 2023].

7 Interview with the author, 3 August 2023.

8 Interview with the author, 30 August 2023.

9 Interview with the author, 7 July 2023.

10 Interview with the author, 27 June 2023. Includes all subsequent quotes from Tony Shrimplin.

11 'Tales of Old Soho', *AnOther*, 15 May 2014, https://www.another-mag.com/art-photography/3619/tales-of-old-soho [accessed 18 August 2023].

Notes

12 The Gentle Author, 'The Huguenots of Soho', *Spitalfields Life*, 12 June 2015 https://spitalfieldslife.com/2015/06/12/huguenot-soho/ [accessed 18 August 2023].

13 Interview with the author, 9 July 2023.

14 Interview with the author, 3 July 2023. Includes all subsequent quotes from Paul Willetts.

15 'The Windmill Theatre, Great Windmill Street, London, W.1', *arthurlloyd.co.uk*, http://www.arthurlloyd.co.uk/WindmillTheatre.htm [accessed 18 August 2023].

16 Paul Willetts, *Members Only: The Life and Times of Paul Raymond* (London: Serpent's Tail, 2010), pp. 411–12.

17 *Ibid.*, pp. 310–11.

18 Interview with the author, 26 June 2023. Includes all subsequent quotes from Andrew Daniel.

19 Interview with the author, 11 November 2021.

20 *Ibid.*

21 *Soft Cell's Non-Stop Exotic Video Show* [video], dir. Tim Pope (London: Picture Music International, 1982).

22 Interview with the author, 12 June 2023.

23 Peter Holt, 'Police raid on Soft Cell's offices', *Evening Standard*, 15 June 1982.

24 Almond, *Tainted Life*, p. 134.

25 Interview with the author, 12 June 2023.

26 *Soft Cell's Non-Stop Exotic Video Show*.

27 Betty Page [Beverley Glick], 'Marc Almond: the human torch', *NOISE!*, 8 July 1982.

28 Interview with the author, 11 November 2021.

29 Interview with the author, 9 November 2021.

30 'Shame' [TV sketch], *Not the Nine O'Clock News*, televised on BBC2, 8 March 1982.

31 'Why Marc was all a-quiver', *Evening Standard*, 7 June 1982, p. 17.

32 Interview with the author, 19 July 2023.

33 Interview with the author, 2 June 2023.

34 Matthew Lindsay, 'Sex music for gargoyles: Soft Cell's *The Art of Falling Apart*', *The Quietus*, 12 December 2013, https://thequietus.com/articles/14100-soft-cell-interview-marc-almond [accessed 18 August 2023].

35 Bob Gourley, 'Marc Almond interviewed about his solo career and time with Soft Cell', *Chaos Control Digizine*, 1 March 1999,

https://chaoscontrol.com/marc-almond/ [accessed 27 August 2023].

36 Interview with the author, 11 August 2023.
37 Lindsay, 'Sex music for gargoyles'.
38 Joyce Purnick, 'City closes bar frequented by homosexuals, citing sexual activity linked to AIDS', *New York Times*, 19 November 1985.
39 Interview with the author, 21 April 2023.
40 Mark Fisher, 'Marc Almond: from bedsit to plague pit', *Guardian*, 18 July 2011, https://www.theguardian.com/stage/2011/jul/18/marc-almond-interview-ten-plagues [accessed 27 August 2023].
41 Blah Snarto, 'Coil – Tainted Love [HQ]' [video], YouTube, uploaded 24 April 2009, https://www.youtube.com/watch?v=4GUnUGK gWDY [accessed 18 August 2023].
42 Lindsay, 'Sex music for gargoyles'.
43 Steve Sutherland, 'The art of staying together', *Melody Maker*, 15 January 1983.
44 Interview with the author, 19 July 2023.
45 Interview with the author, 12 June 2023.
46 Simon Tebbutt, 'Rise and fall', *Record Mirror*, 8 January 1983.
47 Paul Colbert, 'Where the art is', *Melody Maker*, 23 January 1983.
48 Interview with the author, 2 June 2023.
49 'Soft Cell versus Phonogram', *Melody Maker*, 12 March 1983, p. 5.
50 Interview with the author, 12 June 2023.

9 We could go out to dinner but we're always on drugs

1 David Keenan, *England's Hidden Reverse: A Secret History of the Esoteric Underground*, revised and expanded edn (London: Strange Attractor, 2022), pp. 48–52.
2 Interview with the author, 14 September 2023. Includes all further quotations from Philip Hoare.
3 Interview with the author, 11 July 2023. Includes all further quotations from JG Thirlwell.
4 Interview with the author, 30 August 2023.
5 Interview with the author, 11 August 2023.
6 Interview with the author, 21 August 2023. Includes all further quotations from Martin McCarrick.

7 Interview with the author, 3 August 2023.

8 *Ibid.*

9 Interview with the author, 9 August 2023. Includes all subsequent quotes from Billy McGee.

10 Interview with the author, 3 August 2023.

11 *Ibid.*

12 Wesley Doyle, *Conform to Deform: The Weird and Wonderful World of Some Bizzare* (London: Jawbone, 2022), p. 117.

13 Interview with the author, 24 August 2023. Includes all subsequent quotes from Anne Stephenson.

14 Interview with the author, 21 August 2023. Includes all further quotations from Gini Ball.

15 Interview with the author, 3 August 2023.

16 *Ibid.*

17 *Ibid.*

18 *Ibid.*

19 *Ibid.*

20 Interview with the author, 23 March 2023.

21 Interview with the author, 11 August 2023.

22 Interview with the author, 3 August 2023.

23 Ray Moseley, 'Spain's drug habit the price of liberty', *Chicago Tribune*, 11 May 1986.

24 Interview with the author, 13 August 2023. Includes all subsequent quotes from Gary Barnacle.

25 Interview with the author, 12 June 2023.

26 *Ibid.*

27 Interview with the author, 30 August 2023.

28 Almond, *Tainted Life*, p. 214.

29 Chris Bohn, 'Love amongst the ruined', *New Musical Express*, 12 November 1983, pp. 44–5.

30 *Ibid.*

31 Interview with the author, 14 July 2023.

32 Almond, *Tainted Life*, p. 234.

33 Lindsay, 'Sex music for gargoyles'.

34 Interview with the author, 12 June 2023.

35 Ball, *Electronic Boy*, p. 179.

36 Jim Reid, 'Mamba's enclosure', *Record Mirror*, 13 August 1983.

37 Interview with the author, 12 June 2023.

Notes

38 Simon Tebbutt, 'Soft Cell "split" shocker', *Record Mirror*, 20 August 1983.

39 Almond, *Tainted Life*, p. 207.

40 Tebbutt, 'Soft Cell "split" shocker'.

41 *Ibid.*

42 Bohn, 'Love amongst the ruined'.

43 Interview with the author, 30 August 2023.

44 Interview with the author, 12 June 2023.

45 Interview with the author, 2 June 2023.

46 Interview with the author, 23 March 2023.

47 Adam Sweeting, 'The vice presidents', *Melody Maker*, 17 March 1984.

48 Tony Mitchell, 'Gomorrah's world', *Sounds*, 24 March 1984, p. 37.

49 Paul Morley, 'Sodom all', *New Musical Express*, 17 March 1984, p. 33.

50 Adam Sweeting, 'Torment in Torremolinos', *Melody Maker*, 21 January 1984.

51 Almond, *Tainted Life*, p. 237.

52 Interview with the author, 2 June 2023.

53 *Ibid.*

INDEX

Arnold, Tim 110, 160–163
    passim
Art of Falling Apart, The
    artwork 178–179
    critical reception 183–184
    promotion 200
    recording 153, 176–177
    sound 184
Ashworth, Peter 80, 166–168
    passim, 178–179, 188,
    201

'Baby Doll' 179
Ball, Gini 192–193 *passim*,
    197–201 *passim*, 215,
    218
Barrett, Norman 13–14 *passim*,
    20
Barnacle, Gary 200, 202–203
    passim, 215–216, 218
Basic Design 22, 25
Batcave, the 191–193, 196,
    198
Beatles, the 19, 24
Beck Road, Hackney 186–189

'Bedsitter' 6, 61, 98, 118–120
Bell, Colin 100, 108, 115–116
    passim, 182–183, 195,
    212
Blackpool 5–6, 60, 62–63
    Golden Mile 13
    Highland Room at Blackpool
        Mecca 18, 87, 89–91,
        94, 96
    music scene and discos 9, 18
    Pleasure Beach 6, 18–21
    Tower and Tower Circus
        12–14
Blitz Club, the 66–70, 82, 128,
    133
Blue, Ruza 132–134
Boch, Richard, 127, 129,
    136–138 *passim*, 180
Bolan, Marc 17, 109
Bowie, David 67, 69, 155, 198
    influence on Soft Cell 17,
        109, 154, 175
    musical experimentation 37,
        64
    sexuality 110–111, 115

Index

Brassey, Pamina 128–130 *passim*, 136–140 *passim*

Brill, Dianne 126–127 *passim*, 131, 138, 143, 148–149 *passim*

Burnham, Hugo 33–35 *passim*, 41, 52–56 *passim*

Buzzcocks 56–58

Cabaret 32, 34
Cabaret Futura 71–73, 82
Cabaret Voltaire (band)
  collaborations with Soft Cell members 205, 208
  innovations with synthesisers 3, 65
  influence on Soft Cell 59
  work with Some Bizzare 78, 79, 188
Camden Palace 71, 157, 191–192
Cave, Nick 191–192, 205, 206, 215
CBGB 129, 130
clowns 14–17
Charnley, James 24–26 *passim*
Curtis, Colin 18, 90–94 *passim*

Danceteria 129, 133, 142–144, 148–149, 165, 206
Daniel, Andrew 163–164 *passim*
Darling, John 24, 36–37, 76, 117
Depeche Mode 66, 72, 82, 174, 220
  contribution to *Some Bizzare Album* 75–76, 187

Dewhirst, Ian 47–49 *passim*, 81–82, 88–95 *passim*, 97–100 *passim*
DJing
  in Blackpool 9, 19
  in hip hop 132
  in Leeds 47–49
  in New York 135–138
  in Northern Soul 18, 90, 93, 95–96, 97
  remixing 150–151
  Stevo's avant-garde sets 74–75, 173
drugs
  amphetamines 89, 199, 201–202, 207, 208
  cannabis 164, 199, 209
  cocaine 139, 178, 208, 219
  decriminalisation in Spain 202
  during recording sessions 144–146, 151, 200
  ecstasy 121–124, 139, 147, 151, 157, 169
  heroin 164, 180, 207, 208
  inhalants 207
  LSD 154–155, 173, 178, 182
  mescaline 178, 202
  in New York 121, 125, 139
  in the Northern Soul scene 90–91

early electronic music 37, 64–67, 76
Ecstasy, Cindy 169–170, 175, 178
  contributions in songs and videos 152, 178
  in New York 125, 138–139, 169–170

Index

relationship with Marc Almond 120, 121, 175, 178
Egan, Rusty 67–71 *passim*, 81, 133, 155, 157–158
Ellis, Ron 19
Eno, Brian 37, 64–65

Fad Gadget *see* Tovey, Frank
fame 112–113, 116–117, 125–126
   in America 143, 207
   relationship with fans 112, 189–190
fashion 11, 49–51, 67–70, 92–93
F Club, the 41–43, 52
Feather, Huw 10–12 *passim*, 15–16 *passim*, 20–21 *passim*, 31–32, 60, 83, 165, 167–173 *passim*, 208
Fenton, the 41, 53
Ferry, Dr Katherine 5–9 *passim*
Foetus *see* Thirlwell, JG
Fritscher, Jack 127, 131–132 *passim*, 140–141 *passim*, 180
'Frustration' 59, 169
Futurama Festival 63–64

gay culture
   AIDS crisis 180–181, 183
   clubs 43–44, 70, 114, 140–141, 157, 180
   cruising 12
   homophobia 51–52, 111–116
   in Marc Almond's clothing and image 108–111
   in the music industry 114–116, 150
   in New York 131
   in Soho 158–159
Geesin, Ron 26
Gilroy, Darla-Jane 67–70 *passim*
'Girl with the Patent Leather Face, The' 76
Gittins, Ian 105–106, 112
Glick, Beverley 75, 100–101 *passim*, 114, 122, 125–126, 177
Goldberg, Harvey 125–127 *passim*, 130, 146–148, 176
goth 111
Gould, Roy 106–107 *passim*
Griffith, Steven 59, 61

Hardwick-Allen, Tom 16
hip hop 132–135, 137, 145
Hoare, Philip 186–189 *passim*
Hogan, Annie 33–34, 46, 52, 61–63 *passim*, 80, 102, 105, 113–114 *passim*, 122, 154–155, 157, 189, 215
   DJing 48, 103, 200
   playing with the Mambas 191–201 *passim*
Human League, the 48, 59, 64, 65–66, 220
   League Unlimited Orchestra 150
Immaculate Consumptive, the 205–207

Index

independent record labels
  Big Frock Rekords 58–59
  importance in Northern Soul
    94
  Motown 18
  Mute 66, 75
  New York labels 134–135
  Operation Twilight 186–187
  punk labels 57–59
In Strict Tempo 208

Johnson, Matt 158, 194

Keenan, John 41–43 *passim*,
    63, 100
'Kitchen Sink Drama' 179
Kraftwerk 18–19, 38, 50, 67, 87

Leeds
  Chapeltown 30, 42
  Polytechnic 15, 22–23, 40
  University of 33
Levine, Ian 18, 89–97 *passim*,
    100, 157
'Loving You, Hating Me' 185
Lunch, Lydia, 190, 192, 205–206

McCarrick, Martin 188–189,
    191–192, 197–204
    passim
McGee, Billy 190, 197–204
    passim, 206–207
    passim, 212–213, 218
Marc and the Mambas 199,
    221–222
  formation 193–195
  live performances 196,
    201–202, 213
  split 211–213

Torment and Toreros 197,
    209–210
  Untitled 194–196
'Martin' 59, 179, 181, 183, 219
Mediasound studios 123,
    144–148, 153, 176
'Memorabilia' 80–82, 85,
    98–99, 121, 190, 218
  Non-Stop Ecstatic Dancing
    remix 151–152
Miller, Daniel 75, 80–81 *passim*,
    98–99, 136, 151
  recordings as the Normal 66
Mineshaft, the 140–141, 180
Moss, Brian 49, 52, 83, 100,
    102–103 *passim*, 112,
    122, 124, 139, 147
Mutant Moments 58–60, 77,
    80
Mudd Club, the 136–137

National Front, the 50, 52–54
Neate, Chris 43–44, 46–51
    passim, 62, 156
New Romantics 50, 70, 75, 81,
    84, 128
New York
  decline in the 1970s
    127–129
  LGBTQ+ scene 131–132,
    140–141
  nightlife 121–125,
    129–130, 132–134,
    148–149, 157
Non-Stop Erotic Cabaret
  artwork 154, 165–166, 168,
    178
  critical reception 149–150,
    183

Index

launch party 148–149
Non-Stop Ecstatic Dancing
    150–152, 169
Non-Stop Exotic Video Show
    168–173
recording 145–148
Northern Soul 18–19, 87–97,
    107, 127, 151, 165, 221
Numan, Gary 37, 65–66, 132
'Numbers' 179, 181, 183–184
Nuttall, Jeff 24–28, 29, 36, 54,
    117
    Bomb Culture 24–25

Parkin, Sophie 26–27 *passim*,
    51, 53, 68–69, 156
Parry, Steve 64–65 *passim*, 76
Phonogram 85, 114–115, 118,
    151, 195, 215, 217, 220
    creative interventions 98–99,
        106–108, 182–183
    disputes with Soft Cell 100,
        106, 120, 173, 176–177
    vandalism of Phonogram
        office 184–185
    signing of Soft Cell 77–78,
        80
Piper, Rudolf 129, 142–143
    passim
Pope, Tim, 118, 154, 168–174
    passim
P-Orridge, Genesis 39, 78, 186,
    188, 208
Psychic TV 78, 186, 188, 190,
    204, 215
punk
    influence on Soft Cell and
        associates 56, 58, 78,
        171, 192–193

scene in Leeds 41, 50–51, 54
scene in New York 126–127
Sex Pistols, the 55–56
Ratcliffe, Jackie 14
Raymond, Paul 154, 161–163
relationships with press 84,
    113, 166, 177, 182,
    184–185, 205, 221
    album reviews 149–150,
        183–184, 209, 216
    conflict with *Record Mirror*
        and fallout 209–213
    live reviews 35, 63, 217
    'Sex Dwarf' scandal 171–172
    Stevo's futurist chart 75–76
Rocky Horror Picture Show, The
    32, 56
Rolink, Jane 173, 189, 191,
    199

Sarko, Anita 137–138, 176
'Say Hello, Wave Goodbye'
    119, 147, 150, 190, 194,
    218
seaside in Britain
    history 5–10, 20–21
    influence on Soft Cell and
        associates 6, 11–12, 21
Second World War 8, 24, 68,
    131, 159
'Seedy Films' 147, 165, 168,
    169
'Sex Dwarf' 115, 147, 151
    music video and controversy
        170–174, 222
sex work 35, 43, 148, 154, 159,
    164, 170, 173
Sherlock, Steve 197, 199, 212
Shrimplin, Tony 158, 165

Index

Sioux, Siouxsie 40, 42, 56, 63,
        154–155, 192, 193, 196
Soho
    geography 164–165
    history 159–160
    influence on Soft Cell 60,
        153–154, 165–167
    nightlife 158, 191–193,
        221
    sex industry 154–155,
        160–161
Some Bizzare
    offices in Trident Studios 155,
        171, 187–190, 193
    signees and employees 79,
        173, 187–189, 190,
        192, 197, 208
    Some Bizzare Album 75–76,
        77, 220
Southport 5, 10
    fairground 11, 21
    Floral Hall 17
    gay scene 12
    music scene 19
    Theatre 11–12
Stephenson, Anne 192–193,
        196, 199, 212, 213
Stevo 117, 125, 155, 158, 171,
        173–174, 203
    early years as DJ and chart
        compiler 74–76
    house in Hammersmith 191
    management of Soft Cell
        77–78, 208, 212–213,
        214, 222
    negotiations with major labels
        78–80, 187–188
    smashing of Phonogram's
        office 184–185

Strange, Richard 71–73 passim,
        82, 114
student art and performances
    debut Soft Cell show at Leeds
        Polytechnic 40
    Deterioration 15
    Glamour In Squalor 30
    Senseless 28–30
    sound experiments 36,
        37–38
    Teenage Vice 30
    theatre shows 34
    Twilights and Lowlifes 39
    Vampire Cat of Nabéshima,
        The 31
    Zazou 35, 39
Studio 54 121, 128, 129, 133,
        140, 143
Suicide (band) 3, 38, 40, 41,
        84, 117, 136, 199
Sutcliffe, Peter 53–54
synthesisers 36–37, 65–66, 72,
        82, 99, 102, 146, 181

'Tainted Love'
    Coil version 181
    Gloria Jones version 87–88,
        95–99, 119
    Soft Cell version
        commercial success 103,
            111–112, 118–119,
            121, 125, 173, 176,
            220–221
        demo with Daniel Miller 99
        exclusion from setlists 207,
            219
        music video 169, 172
        performances on Top of the
            Pops 17, 106–111, 113

Index

reception 149, 190
recording 101–103
re-release with 'Numbers'
  184–185
Teasdale, Geoff 23–29 *passim*,
  36
Thee Temple ov Psychick Youth
  186, 188–189
The The 76, 78, 187, 194–195,
  198
This Last Night ... In Sodom
  214–219
  reception 216
Thirlwell, JG 79, 187–191
  passim, 195, 197–199
  passim, 201, 205–207
  passim, 215
Thorne, Mike 99, 101–102
  passim, 123, 144–148
  passim, 151, 176, 182
Throbbing Gristle 38–39, 43,
  59, 75, 84, 117, 173
Tilby, Anne 26–27 *passim*,
  31–33 *passim*, 38, 44,
  56
Top of the Pops 17, 103,
  105–113, 170

'Torch' 119, 170, 176, 178,
  183, 190
Tovey, Frank 32–33, 36, 65–66

Unsworth, Cathi 111

Vicious Pink 42, 49, 123
visual identity 11, 59–60, 83,
  165–167

Warden, Josephine 42, 49, 55,
  60, 62, 102–103, 119,
  123–124, 139, 147,
  180
Warehouse, the 44–48, 50, 54,
  61, 62, 80, 82, 97–98,
  112, 139, 156
Warhol, Andy 71, 144, 148, 149
Wershba, Don 126, 144–147
  passim
Wiand, Dino 45–47, 50
Wiand, Mike 44–48 *passim*, 50,
  97, 100, 116
Willetts, Paul 159–163 *passim*
Wilson, Mari 158